Parents, Early Years and Learning

Parents, Early Years and Learning

Parents as Partners
in the Early Years Foundation Stage –
Principles into Practice

Helen Wheeler and Joyce Connor,
with additional material by Heather Goodwin

Published by the National Children's Bureau

National Children's Bureau, 8 Wakley Street, London EC1V 7QE
Tel: 0207 843 6000
Website: www.ncb.org.uk
Registered charity number: 258825

NCB works in partnership with Children in Scotland
(www.childreninscotland.org.uk) and Children in Wales
(www.childreninwales.org.uk).

© National Children's Bureau 2009

ISBN: 978-1-905818-43-3

British Library Cataloguing in Publication Data
A catalogue record for this book is available from the British Library

uced for non-commercial education or

source is acknowledged.

of the authors and not necessarily those

ı, Wales.

Contents

Acknowledgements

We would like to thank all those who helped with the content of this book, the original design and development of PEAL training and materials 2005–07, and the roll-out of national training 2005–08. Please see Appendix 3 for details of the PEAL team.

Thanks to the many families who agreed to contribute their stories and images, including contributions to 'Parents' voices' from *Growing Together at the Pen Green Centre: Training Resources,* and the use of photographs from the Parents' Centre, Coram Family.

Finally, we are also grateful to all staff members in the Early Childhood Unit and partner organisations who helped with the roll-out of training and the revision of materials, and to Gill Haynes, Kim Bevan and all those who worked in the Accreditation Team.

Helen Wheeler and Joyce Connor

1 Introduction

This book is about working with parents as partners in their young children's learning and development.

The book arises from the work of PEAL (Parents, Early Years and Learning). PEAL was commissioned by the Department for Education and Skills (DfES) and developed in 2005–07 by a small team at the Early Childhood Unit of the National Children's Bureau (NCB) in partnership with Coram Family and the London Borough of Camden. PEAL reviewed literature and research, gathered examples of successful practice from the early years sector, and delivered a national training programme for teachers and other early years practitioners to support parental involvement in young children's learning. The training programme was extended through further funding from the Department for Children, Schools and Families (DCSF) as part of the Early Learning Partnerships Project 2007–08.

This book updates and complements the *PEAL Reader*, making it available to a wider audience beyond those attending the training. It revisits much of the original material and includes learning from the training delivery itself. Extracts from the original PEAL practice examples are highlighted and new parent-partnership projects are introduced, gathered from practitioners in children's centres who attended PEAL training in its first year. Reflections on the design, delivery and impact of the training are also included in Section 8.

The principle of working with parents to involve them in their children's learning is firmly established within national policy. The Children's Plan (2007) emphasises parents' support for their child's learning as an essential foundation for achievement. Parents, during consultation, asked for more involvement in their children's education. The good practice that already exists in many early years settings is recognised in the plan but the need to reach out and involve all parents is emphasised.

All settings offering early years provision are required to deliver the Early Years Foundation Stage (EYFS) from September 2008. This sets out detailed principles, requirements and guidance on working with all parents as partners in learning. These are outlined in Section 2 of this book. Subsequent sections then look at the evidence base for the principles and requirements, and at how settings can work towards creating real partnership with parents – putting the principles into practice.

PEAL provides a framework for practice. It outlines key underpinning elements that need to be in place for successful partnership, and advocates sharing research and practice with parents. It is not, however, a prescribed method. It does not try to set out exactly what should happen in a setting or school, or what educational theory or practice should be shared. It provides a foundation and encourages self-reflection – both as individual practitioners and as teams of professionals working with families.

PEAL suggests that settings should think through what they do well already, include parents in this process, and consider what could be enhanced and improved. It points to a wide range of practical ways of working, and encourages practitioners to make their own choices, know their own communities well and have confidence in developing partnership in ways that match their families' needs.

The importance of working more effectively with parents to involve them in learning cannot be overstated. Just as the EYFS works to end the artificial distinction between childcare and education, partnership with parents acts to end the distinction between home and school as sites of learning. Children learn from everything they experience, wherever they are and whoever they are with. The greater the continuity between home and setting, and the richer the learning environment in both, the more children will benefit.

The impact of taking the time out to read, reflect and plan future practice is illustrated by some quotes from participants following PEAL training:

- "It's given me hope about what my setting does with parents, but also how we can improve and develop."

- "I came here today knowing that I am quite good at working with parents, but now I realise I only scratch the surface."

- "I feel we are meeting the needs of families well, but there is always room to move forward and there are some wonderful ideas here."

- "PEAL has made me think a lot – I'm excited about starting to use some of the ideas."

- "It's re-motivated me and given me more starting points."

It is hoped that this book will assist more practitioners to examine their practice, encourage them to seek further training, and feel excited at the prospect of embedding partnership with parents more firmly into their settings and services.

What is PEAL?

PEAL inspires and supports all those working with young children and their families to encourage greater parental involvement in early learning and development through evidence-based training and a pack of supporting materials. This includes a *Training Guide, Reader,* self-evaluation questions, a DVD and illustrative practice examples.

PEAL provides a day's facilitated training, and includes up to one day's preparation activities. Accreditation is available at Level 3 through City and Guilds. To date nearly 5,000 practitioners have attended the one-day training from a wide range of settings and services, including childminders. PEAL has also funded 24 practice development projects in children's centres across all regions of England and developed training for local authority teams to support strategic planning for parental involvement in learning.

The training is available from NCB and through local authorities (and more information can be found at www.peal.org.uk).

Definition of terms

Parent(s)
The term 'parent' or 'parents' is intended to refer to mothers and fathers as well as any member of the extended family, foster carers or other persons, male or female, who have the responsibility of caring for a child. Any regular carer of a child has a major and direct impact on a child's learning and development.

Practitioner
The term 'practitioner' is used to denote anyone working in an early years setting who has regular contact with children and responsibility for their learning, development and care. Many of the ideas are also relevant to those working in an outreach or family support capacity. A variety of terms are used in the examples of practice – teachers, nursery nurses, workers, childminders, educators and so on – reflecting the language used and recognised by the settings providing the examples.

Key person
The term 'key person' is used to denote a practitioner who has special responsibility for working with a small group of children in a setting. The terms 'key worker', 'key carer' and 'family worker' appear in the examples of practice contributed by settings.

Setting
The term 'setting' is used to denote any early years setting providing part-time or full-time learning, development and care to children, but a range of other titles are used – such as children's centre, nursery, nursery school, preschool, childminder, early excellence centre or playgroup. This reflects the current variety of settings in existence and, sometimes, the preferences of those contributing material.

Partnership
It is possible to work in partnership with parents in many ways – for instance, in the original design of buildings and services, in the recruitment of staff, in direct delivery of services or in the active management of centres. PEAL has a particular focus, which involves looking at how practitioners can work in partnership with parents in order to support more parental involvement in their children's learning and development, both in early years settings and at home.

2 The Early Years Foundation Stage: Parents as partners

This section looks at what the Early Years Foundation Stage (EYFS) says about working in partnership with parents in children's learning.

The EYFS aims to raise the quality of education and care in all early childhood settings for children from birth to five (end of Reception). Individual practitioners and settings are required to examine practice and reflect on their work with young children and families in the light of a set of guiding principles and practice commitments. These are grouped into the themes:

- A Unique Child

- Positive Relationships

- Enabling Environments

- Learning and Development.

| **Principles** | ideas/beliefs that underpin practice. |
| **Commitments** | describe how principles can be put into practice. |

The principles and commitments include the recognition that all areas of development are connected to each other and are equally important. Children learn from birth, in the context of loving and secure relationships, and develop in individual ways and at varying rates. Plans for learning and development should be based on careful observation of children's individual needs and interests. All children are entitled to safe, stimulating, inclusive environments, both indoors and out. They learn through active, purposeful play – with people, objects, ideas and events that engage and involve them – sometimes for sustained periods. They benefit from a balance of adult-led and child-initiated activities and from adults who provide rich experience and interact in ways that encourage the development of language, thinking skills and creativity.

Positive Relationships

The focus of this book is to look at the relationship between parents and practitioners within the theme of Positive Relationships – in particular Commitment 2.2 to view parents as partners in young children's learning and development.

The commitments to practice within this theme are:

2.1 Respecting Each Other: Every interaction is based on caring professional relationships and respectful acknowledgement of the feelings of children and their families.

2.2 Parents as Partners: Parents are children's first and most enduring educators. When parents and practitioners work together in early years settings, the results have a positive impact on children's development and learning.

2.3 Supporting Learning: Warm, trusting relationships with knowledgeable adults support children's learning more effectively than any amount of resources.

2.4 Key Person: A key person has special responsibilities for working with a small number of children, giving them the reassurance to feel safe and cared for and building relationships with their parents.

Each of these commitments has a corresponding card containing additional information, key messages and prompt questions. The cards, along with the *Practice Guidance,* provide a starting point for reflection on how to put the principles into practice.

Statutory Framework

More detail in support of Commitment 2.2 is contained within the *Statutory Framework*. Here are two key extracts.

1.16 Introduction – A principled approach

Creating the framework for partnership working

The text reads:

> "Close working between early years practitioners and parents is vital for the identification of children's learning needs and to ensure a quick response to any area of particular difficulty. Parents and families are central to a child's well being and practitioners should support this important relationship by sharing information and offering support for extending learning in the home."

2.19 The learning and development requirements

The assessment arrangements

Practitioners should make assessments and plan for children's future development and learning through regular observation. The text reads:

> "Assessments should be based on practitioners' observations of what children are doing in their day-to-day activities. As judgements are based on observational evidence gathered from a wide range of learning and teaching contexts, it is expected that all adults who interact with the child should contribute to the process, and that account will be taken of information provided by parents. An essential feature of parental involvement is an ongoing dialogue, building on the partnership begun by any previous practitioner(s). Settings should report progress and achievements to parents throughout the EYFS."

In summary, to work in partnership with parents, early years settings should:

- Acknowledge parents as a child's first and most enduring educators.

- Assign a key person to each child who should work to form a warm, trusting, respectful relationship with that child and their family.

- Work with parents to enhance learning and development – establish an ongoing dialogue with parents, share information, take account of parents' own observations of their child and support learning in the home.

These then are the expectations of the EYFS. There is conclusive research and practice evidence that these commitments and requirements are central to improving the quality of education and care for all children. The following sections outline this evidence in some detail and then go on to explore what effective work with parents looks like – that is, how do settings put these principles and commitments into practice?

Section 3 begins by exploring the specific commitment to acknowledge parents as a child's first and most enduring educators. Why is this so important for children's intellectual and social development?

3 Why work with parents?

Parents are a child's first and most enduring educators. Parents and families are the most important people in children's lives. They have the greatest influence over them, particularly in their early years. What parents do at home with their very young babies and children has a major impact on social, emotional and intellectual development.

The Effective Provision of Pre-School Education study (EPPE) followed 3,000 children from the ages of three to seven and found that the quality of the home learning environment provided by parents has a greater impact upon learning and development than parents' education level, occupation or incomes. A key conclusion of the study is set out in the following heading.

'What parents do is more important than who parents are'

Parents who report regularly undertaking activities that engage and 'stretch a child's mind' contribute markedly positive effects to their child's development. Their children are already ahead in both social and intellectual development at the age of three – showing advanced language ability, higher levels of confidence, cooperation and sociability as well as having greater discrimination and spatial skills (recognising similarities in pictures, completing patterns and block building).

The advantage continues as these children progress through school. They continue to perform well on language and discrimination tasks and show greater awareness of rhyme and alliteration, written symbols and early number concepts. At age seven they attain more highly on standardised reading and maths tests as well as expressing more positive attitudes towards learning (Sylva and others 2004).

The following types of home learning activities, as reported by parents, were found to have the greatest significance:

- reading with and to children

- going on visits

- making opportunities to play with friends

- playing with letters and numbers

- going to the library

- singing songs and rhymes

- drawing and painting.

The message is a powerful one. Social class, income, living conditions and parents' own education levels clearly are directly related to child development outcomes. Every Child Matters (DfES 2003a) highlights research showing a big gap between the development of children from different socio-economic groups. Children from disadvantaged backgrounds show less ability as early as 22 months in a range of assessments of language and cognitive development (Feinstein 1999).

The EPPE research, however, demonstrates that the quality of the home learning environment can act as a significant modifying factor. Parents may live in disadvantaged circumstances and may not have achieved well educationally, but if they regularly engage in activities that help to encourage thinking and 'stretch a child's mind' as part of everyday life at home in the early years, they can enhance their child's progress and development.

The EPPE research gives two additional striking findings. First, children in the study at age seven were less likely to have assessments for special educational needs if their parents reported having engaged regularly in home learning activities. Secondly, boys were less likely to have the benefit of these high quality home learning experiences than girls; parents seem to do less of these activities with their very young boys. The reasons for the second finding are uncertain. It might well be that boys are harder to engage or choose to participate less in these activities; or that parents have different expectations of boys' and girls' behaviour – or a mixture of both. It is, however, important for both parents and practitioners to be aware of this in the light of boys' relative educational underachievement.

Follow-up interviews have been conducted with 21 families from the original EPPE sample (across five ethnic groups), all of whom have children with good educational attainment and who had provided positive early home learning environments despite living in disadvantaged circumstances. The findings highlight how wide a range of family members – including grandparents, other extended family and older siblings – provide support for learning. All the families had read regularly with their young children, as well as providing other stimulating activities. Additional common factors include a general awareness of the benefits of education and a belief that action can be taken, by both parents and children, that leads to greater educational achievement (Sylva and others 2007).

Other research confirms the positive influence of the early home learning environment. Desforges reviewed a wide range of studies (including EPPE) and concluded that what parents do at home 'has a significant positive effect on children's achievement and adjustment even after all other factors shaping attainment have been taken out of the equation' (Desforge 2003, p.4).

Blanden (2006) used data from the British Cohort Study (a sample of 18,000 people born in the same week in 1970) to look at the main factors enabling children who grow up in low income households to 'buck the trend' and escape poverty in later life. High language and cognitive attainment evident as early as five years is seen as a key factor, and parental involvement plays a major role in that attainment. Reading with children is again highlighted as significant.

The effects of parental involvement beyond the age of seven

The EPPE study has been extended (the Effective Provision of Primary Education 3–11) and the same sample of children has been followed through to age 10 (Year 5). At this age the quality of the early home learning environment is still found to be a strong predictor of higher later school attainment (as measured through standardised maths and reading assessments) when all other home background variables are controlled. Parents' qualification level – especially of mothers – is also a strong predictor at this stage (Sammons and others 2007a).

Ongoing parental involvement also continues to have an impact as children progress through primary school. Where primary schools work actively to communicate with parents, children make better academic progress and show better self-regulation (autonomy and confidence in learning). Strong parental support for learning leads to better progress in reading at age 10 and more pro-social behaviour (Sammons and others 2008).

The Desforges review indicates that the positive impact of parental involvement in education is evident across all social classes and ethnic groups and suggests that different levels of parental involvement may even have a greater impact on achievement in the primary age range than the variation in school quality.

Working with parents to enhance the quality of learning taking place at home in the early years is therefore clearly crucial. It enhances children's intellectual and social development and it may also help to build parents' confidence to continue involvement and communication with schools as their children progress through education. (This idea is explored further in a discussion about the nature of partnership in Section 5.)

It is, however, not intended to suggest that enhancing home learning is all that needs to happen to improve children's outcomes. Clear commitments and policies to reduce poverty, improve housing and increase the quality of both early years settings and schools are also necessary. Attending high quality early years provision has been found to have a continuing, positive effect on children's cognitive and social outcomes, and attendance at a highly effective primary school can also moderate the effects of previous poor quality experience. The combination is important. Children who have the advantage of two or more high quality learning environments – from home, preschool or primary school – have added layers of protection against disadvantage (Sammons and others 2007a and b).

Fathers' involvement

It needs to be remembered that the quality of a home learning environment can be influenced by fathers as well as mothers. Goldman (2005) reviewed a wide range of research on fathers' involvement with children aged 4–16. Overall the studies show that fathers who are interested in and get involved in their children's learning, can have a positive impact on both social and emotional development. Their children tend to achieve more at school, have higher expectations and better social outcomes.

A father's involvement has an effect independent of a mother's involvement. If a mother is involved, having a father who gets involved too can give an additional benefit. Some studies show that a father's involvement and interest has a particular impact on boys. Blanden (2006) for instance, found fathers very important for boys' educational outcomes. However, Goldman's (2005) wider review indicates that, overall, research findings on this are mixed.

Why is the impact of home learning in the early years so strong?

Desforges summarises the influence of home as 'enduring, pervasive and direct'. Parents have not only the first but also the most long-lasting effect upon children. They have the closest continuous relationship; their influence is immediate and woven into every aspect of daily life. Children receive not just skills, knowledge and intellectual stimulation at home; they can also absorb a positive attitude towards learning and a strong self-image as a successful learner.

Learning at home clearly has many advantages. Parents know their children very well. They know more about their interests, previous experience and understandings. Parents are 'tuned into' their child and can respond more effectively, helping their child make sense of experiences and connect one experience to another. Children can take more initiative and direct their own learning at home, asking questions as part of everyday life (Siraj-Blatchford and McCallum 2005).

Parents at home have more opportunity to model behaviour and practice, giving closer individual attention; and learning can be shaped to meet a child's immediate interests and needs. Adults and older siblings can respond to real rather than contrived situations so that learning seems effortless and spontaneous (Hannon 1995).

Whalley and the Pen Green Team (2001) studied video of parent–child interactions and noticed how well parents recall and relate past experience to what a child is doing or saying 'now'; verbally reflect back to a child what they are doing; extend experience by showing new approaches; give time for exploration of a child's interests; ask for a child's views and feelings; encourage the making of choices and decisions; know when to step in or allow their child to 'have a go'; and intuitively sense what their child needs next either physically or emotionally.

Early learning within close relationships at home is then very powerful and it appears to be particularly important for children's very early development. Babies and young children who are listened to and share talking, singing and play activities that encourage them to think within their home, everyday environment have an early marked intellectual and social advantage.

Research sheet 1 summarises some of the key research findings, which have considerable implications for early years practice. All those working with young children and their families need not only to appreciate and acknowledge the central importance of the home environment on early learning but also to think through how to share research with parents constructively and positively – and support families in their role as educators of their own children.

Research sheet 1: Why involve parents in their children's learning?

'What parents do is more important than who parents are':

- Parents who create high quality home learning environments engage in activities regularly that stretch a child's mind.

- The early home learning environment gives children an advantage in both social and intellectual development.*

- This advantage is already noticeable by age three and continues to seven.

- The early home learning environment has more impact statistically than either social class or parents' own education level.

- Home learning activities could also be viewed as protective factors in reducing the incidence of children receiving assessments for special educational needs (SEN).

- More girls' parents reported engaging in home learning activities than boys'.

- A high quality home learning environment remains a strong predictor of academic attainment at age 10.

    Sources: Sylva and others (2004); Sammons and others (2007a).

Children gain skills at home, but also absorb a positive attitude to and enthusiasm for learning. Parental involvement has an impact across all ethnic groups and social classes. In the primary age range, the impact on achievement of different levels of parental involvement is bigger than differences associated with variations in the quality of schools.
Source: Desforges (2003)

*Social development was analysed in terms of levels of cooperation, confidence, behaviour, and peer sociability. Intellectual development was assessed through tasks:

- Age 3 – verbal comprehension, naming vocabulary, similarities between pictures and block building.

- School entry and end of Reception – similar tasks plus knowledge of the alphabet, rhyme/alliteration and early number concepts.

- End of Years 1 and 2 – assessments included standardised tests of maths and reading, attendance data, special educational needs (SEN) status, and children were asked about their own attitudes to school and learning.

- End of Year 5 – standardised tests of reading and maths.

Adapted from Resource sheet 4.1 PEAL Reader.

As home and family have such a powerful effect on children's early learning and development, it is not surprising that the most effective early years settings and schools – that is, those that achieve the best social and intellectual outcomes for their children – have been found to work closely with parents.

The following sections look at what makes these settings effective. This begins, in Section 4, with a detailed examination of what inhibits parental involvement in learning. Understanding and appreciating how the causal factors interact and combine with each other as barriers to involvement is the first step for practitioners wishing to work more effectively with parents as partners in learning.

4 What stops parental involvement in learning?

There are many factors that often combine to prevent and limit parental involvement in learning. Research sheet 2 on page 21 contains a summary of findings in this area. Some of these factors result from issues and difficulties parents face in their lives, and their past and present experience, beliefs and knowledge; others, however, emanate from the way practitioners and settings communicate and present to parents, how comfortable parents are made to feel and practitioners' own attitudes.

Are some parents just not interested?

Research sheet 2 begins with a firm statement from the team at the Pen Green Centre for Under Fives and Families, that all parents are interested in their child's progress and development. It can sometimes be tempting to blame lack of attendance or response to invitations and initiatives on parents and families themselves – on a general absence of interest in children's progress and education.

This is an assumption that needs firm challenge. The practical experience of individual practitioners and centres such as Pen Green in Northamptonshire and Thomas Coram in the London Borough of Camden, who have specialised in working with parents over many years, shows that it is possible to involve the vast majority of families, and that lack of interest is not one of the major factors standing in the way of parental involvement in learning.

This practical experience on the ground is supported by research. Pen Green's own evaluation of their Parental Involvement Project found that, on average, 84 per cent of parents sustained involvement in their child's learning when offered a flexible range of options for involvement (Whalley and the Pen Green Team 2001). Pugh and De'Ath (1989) examined the nature of partnership with parents in 130 diverse preschool settings and services over a three-year period and found parents were interested in their children's progress and appreciated information. Williams and others (2002) surveyed 2,000 parents with children aged 5–16 and found 58 per cent of parents believe they have equal responsibility for their child's education. Only 2 per cent said it was just the responsibility of school, while 72 per cent of parents said they would welcome more involvement. A recent, larger survey found two-thirds of parents would like to be more involved in their child's education, and the desire to get more involved tended to be stronger among disadvantaged groups. Black and Asian parents were most likely to emphasise parents' responsibility for their child's education (Peters and others 2007). Seaman and others (2006) studied families in four disadvantaged areas in and around Glasgow and concluded that parents have high aspirations for their children based on realistic assessments of their strengths. It is not interest in education that parents lack, but knowledge, information and resources.

Factors that impede involvement

Desforges (2003) comprehensively describes the material and psychological factors that impact on parental involvement levels. Lack of time, pressure from work, living on a low income, single parent status and illness, depression or disability within the family can all stand in the way of active involvement and engagement. Parents may also have little confidence because of their own education level or a history of negative educational experience and memories. They may feel that they cannot make a difference or simply need knowledge of what to do; others may be deterred by a belief that education should really be left to schools, or that intelligence is inherited and cannot be altered to any great degree.

Fathers may be particularly affected by longer working hours, giving less time to spend with their children at home or preventing attendance at events held in the daytime or even early evening. Although more fathers are now involved in the care of their young children, traditional belief systems about fathers as economic providers and mothers as caregivers still have an impact and can affect both parental and practitioner attitudes – particularly towards the care of babies and very young children. Fathers report often feeling invisible to health and children's services professionals. Some fathers can feel particularly uncomfortable and conspicuous coming in to early years settings because of the largely female nature of under fives environments. Men are more likely to feel hesitant about schools and education generally because of negative personal experience (Goldman 2005; Children's Plan 2007).

Draper and Duffy (2006), writing from first-hand experience at Thomas Coram Children's Centre, again highlight time, work pressures and negative memories of school as impediments to involvement, but they also point to how lack of childcare or crèche provision prevents attendance at workshops or events, and how some parents without English as their first language cannot access information or children's records without adequate thought to translation and interpretation. In addition, they point to a lack of a 'shared language' about education that can make communication about learning complex. Different attitudes to and experience of education can make reaching meaningful, shared understandings of how young children learn much more challenging. A common example of this is the challenge involved in explaining to some parents how children learn through active play or conveying the importance of all-year-round outdoor provision. This issue is considered again in Section 5.

These barriers are compounded for minority ethnic families as they are more likely to live in poor housing, to be unemployed or work for very low wages, and fathers have a greater tendency to work long and unpredictable hours. Minority ethnic children are less likely to attend nursery education provision for three and four year olds and their families make less use of formal support services available generally. This pattern may be replicated in early years settings and services – with families making less use of any opportunities and invitations to get involved in children's learning – if linguistic and cultural differences are not thought through adequately and if the existence of racial prejudice and discrimination are not acknowledged. Parents are less likely, for example, to feel comfortable and develop trust in a setting that makes little attempt to reflect their background or represent difference in the make-up of its staff/volunteers, visual displays, equipment or play provision for children (Moran and others 2004; Equalities Review 2007).

For many families the level of basic literacy skills needs to be considered. The Skills for Life Survey (DfES 2003b) found around 16 per cent of adults (over 5 million) with literacy levels at or below Entry Level 3, the expected attainment for 11 year olds (the definition of functional literacy). Some 5 per cent were at or below Level 2, the expected level for 7 year olds. If information about how to help children learn, or advertisements for parent workshops and events, are presented mainly in newsletter or poster format, it will clearly make access very difficult for many families (Leitch Review of Skills 2006).

Parents' experience of services

The Desforges (2003) review indicates that some parents are discouraged from involvement because of their actual experience of communication with practitioners, early years settings, services and schools. Some parents report having been made to feel unwelcome in some way, or state that they are not listened to. Others say their experience leads them to lack trust in professionals.

Pugh and De'Ath (1989) found one of the most common reasons given for non-involvement in preschool settings was feeling unconfident in the face of professional expertise. Parents' attitudes were affected by whether they were made to feel valued and that they had something to offer. They felt that pursuing concerns with staff might make them seem over-anxious and they also worried about staff making critical observations of their parenting skills.

Draper and Duffy (2006) suggest that the quality of the parent–practitioner relationship can be affected by some practitioners holding a view of themselves as 'the expert' on children's learning. This can make it difficult for them to listen actively and to really value parents' views.

The communication and relationship between practitioners and parents may also be affected by practitioner confidence. Some practitioners, even those who are experienced and very competent in work with children, feel uncomfortable and lack confidence in working with parents. As the Pen Green Centre for Under Fives and Families (2004) reminds us: 'Just as parents may feel threatened and nervous when talking to professionals, many professionals feel unsure of their role when talking to parents.' (p16.)

Research sheet 2: What stops involvement?

'We need to begin with the firm belief that all parents are interested in the development and progress of their own children.' (Pen Green Centre for Under Fives and Families 2004)

- Work commitments.

- Time and pressures in busy lives.

- Childcare needs.

- Pressures due to lack of money, illness, disability, single-parent status.

- Own education level; confidence that you can make a difference.

- Knowledge of what to do.

- Negative feelings about schools from own experience.

- Own literacy and numeracy levels poor.

- English not first language.

- Attitudes – 'it's the school's job', 'intelligence is innate'.

- Feeling unwelcome, not trusting teachers.

- Poor experience of other professionals – suspicion of motives.

- Past and ongoing experience of discrimination – race, gender, class, disability, sexual orientation.

- Parents unable to understand or share educational approach.

- Practitioner attitudes – not valuing or listening to parents' view of child.

- Parents not confident in the face of professional expertise.

- Practitioners lacking confidence in talking to parents.

- Practitioners unable to communicate educational approach effectively.

  Sources: Desforges (2003); Draper and Duffy (2006); Harris and Spencer (2000); Whalley and the Pen Green Team (2001).

- 84 per cent of parents at Pen Green were involved in their children's learning when offered a range of options (Whalley and the Pen Green Team 2001).

- 98 per cent of parents surveyed believe they have either equal or some responsibility for their children's education; 58 per cent said equal (Williams and others 2002).

- 67 per cent of parents surveyed want more involvement – especially those in most disadvantaged groups (Peters and others 2007).

- Pugh and De'Ath (1989) found parents interested in their child's progress and appreciated information.

Adapted from Resource sheet 2.1 PEAL Reader.

These then are the main obstacles to parental involvement in their children's learning. Any early years setting or service that wishes to work more effectively with parents should accept that parents are interested in their child's development, take time to think through the main barriers, and seek ways to reduce or overcome as many of these as possible for their parents.

The PEAL framework and training suggests that this process needs to begin with an examination of parent–practitioner relationships in the first instance. This has to be the starting point for any strategy. If practitioners and settings sometimes make parents feel unwelcome, unconfident, undervalued or anxious about being judged then there can be no basis for partnership working or delivery of greater parental involvement. Relationships provide the foundation for encouraging and sustaining parental involvement. This is reflected visually in the PEAL model on page 57 which places relationships at the heart of practice.

The parent voices reproduced on page 23 serve to illustrate how some parents are made to feel by their interactions with practitioners. These are taken from the PEAL *Activities* booklet which participants are asked to consider and work through before attending a training day. Experiences such as these can have a direct and immediate bearing, either positively or negatively, on how much parents feel inclined to get involved, come in to ask questions, share and initiate ideas, respond to invitations or accept home visits.

The EYFS requires the development of respectful relationships with parents. Section 5 considers what this means in more detail, what additional research supports this requirement and what is a respectful relationship?

Parents' voices

Jasbinder, Nila, Niren and Dani's story

Nila is nearly four and the twins are nearly one. When I arrived one morning with Nila at nursery school, the teacher wanted a word because I was getting her in five minutes or so late. She said it was really important to get her there on time. I told her about how hard it is getting out with the twins as well. If one of them needs a nappy change at the last minute I see to them – I have to see to them first as I have to take them to the childminder ready for going on to work. It's twice as likely something will hold us up with the two of them. I felt she was telling me off but I don't think she really understands what my life is like. The teacher asked me why I wasn't reading to Nila for half-an-hour every night. She said it was really important to fit that in. I told her I have to fit things in around getting in after work and getting the meal and getting the babies fed and to bed. I do tell the children stories – often when we're out together, or I try to read to Nila when I can or point out words in the supermarket when we're shopping. It's a case of what's possible at the moment.

Paulina and Raoul's story

When Raoul was in his last few months with his childminder, before leaving to go to nursery school, I thought she would do some visits to the school with him. The school had asked for this and I had tried to do some myself but it was difficult to fit in with work. Every time I made what I thought was a suitable appointment time for the childminder Chrissie, and Raoul to visit, she would cancel it or rearrange it and not go, saying something had cropped up or 'it was such a lovely day I decided to take the children to the park'. I was really disappointed as I thought Chrissie wanted to help me. I don't think she appreciated how difficult it was to take time off as a single working parent. I had to save my holidays for times when Chrissie wasn't available anyway.

Waris and Ahmed's story

Before Ahmed went to Reception class, the nursery school teacher talked to me about how it might feel and what it might be like. We thought about the questions I wanted to ask his new teacher and rang the school to arrange a visit. She went with me and Ahmed to meet his new teacher. We talked about Ahmed – things like what he likes doing, things he might find different to nursery school – and Ahmed showed his new teachers his portfolio. Back at the nursery we talked about how the visit went and what else we could do to help Ahmed. She really made it easier for us to make the move.

Malc and Imogen's story

I started going because I was just curious to see where Linda was taking Imogen and she was just raving about it, said it was a great thing. I went up there and what I liked was the fact that as a male going up, most of these groups tend to be female and child, and I went in there as the father and I'm not made to feel odd at all, it's great. Even the other mothers talk to me, the carers come up and explain things and chat about issues you may not have thought so much about, they talk to you about things and I get a lot out of it as well. It's great to see her playing obviously, I like to follow her around and get involved as well and I'm getting to know a lot of the other kids as well, which is good. They actually come up to me now and offer me toys and things to play with so you really feel part of the group up there, they're really good.

Jenny and Mel's story

I went to collect my daughter from nursery. The nursery worker said she wanted to have a quick word because my daughter had been showing what she felt was some unusual behaviour, running across the room and being completely disruptive and pushing other children. She said she had never seen her behave that way before and just wanted to let me know. I went home feeling very worried but not really knowing what to do about the conversation. I didn't know what I should do about it. A year or two later, she was diagnosed with autism and ADHD [attention deficit hyperactive disorder]. The teacher then said that the nursery staff had always been worried about her learning, about her reading and about her development generally. I hadn't known there were these worries about her learning – only the time when I was told she was being disruptive, they'd never discussed it with me.

Charraine and Kearnu's story

Once I'd given birth to Kearnu they found out I'd got osteoporosis and I'd actually fractured my spine twice so, for a period of three or four months, I couldn't actually lift Kearnu at all. Pen Green Centre really really helps me. They've helped in every way. They get him in and out of the pram for me because they know I can't do it, they're still doing it for me because I've still got a weakness there, and they understand that, and when I go to the groups they look after him for me. They take him round the playgroup itself, they play with all the different toys and it's something I couldn't have done without them. Kearnu wouldn't have had really such a good time because he would've just been sitting at home on his own. So I really don't know where I'd personally be without Pen Green Centre because they've been so wonderful.

Debra and Sam's story

When my child first needed a childminder, I went to see a number to choose one that would suit me. I was a residential worker and worked shifts. Some I looked at seemed to be trying to make our lives fit in with theirs. Then I found this one, and it fitted into our lifestyle and patterns. I also felt I might be missing out on what was happening. The childminder involved me in getting to know what they'd do, gave me an account of a typical day, how they'd go out swimming or to the park and how she believed in learning through play. She knew I'd get a bit anxious and there would be a bit of anxiety about separation and she would acknowledge this. I felt encouraged to ring to see how things were going. I felt I could share what my child had been doing at home. My child could take things in from home – it became a home from home. That was the place with the sort of person I wanted. When my child started nursery I went with the childminder and we both stayed and settled him in. I feel it's important to connect with the person, to see how open they are to questioning and how reassuring they are. Now my son is seven, but my daughter goes to the same childminder.

Azhar and Tazneem's story

We had not long arrived in the country, everything was new. I took my child to the nursery. We didn't know anyone there; it was all different to home. I put my child's name down and they offered her a place the next week. When we came on the first day we went to her peg to hang up her coat. They'd spelled my child's name wrong, so I told them – it's not Tasmin it's Tazneem. The next week something came home with the name spelled wrong again. I thought 'that is not my child's'. I told them again but they kept getting it wrong. It made me feel I don't want to go back again… they don't listen to me or care about my child.

Lisa and Sophie's story

At six weeks it all started with Sophie. She went for a six-week check and found out that she had an ASD and a VSD, which is a hole in the top chambers of her heart and a hole in the bottom, meaning that her heart's enlarged as well because it works harder so she's prone to viruses. That's why she's on the small side as well. It was nice to have some free time to think. I know she's alright with Tracy, Tracy knows what the difference is and I knew she'd be safe but at least I could keep an eye on her. Tracy was probably the only other person she's been with apart from family members.

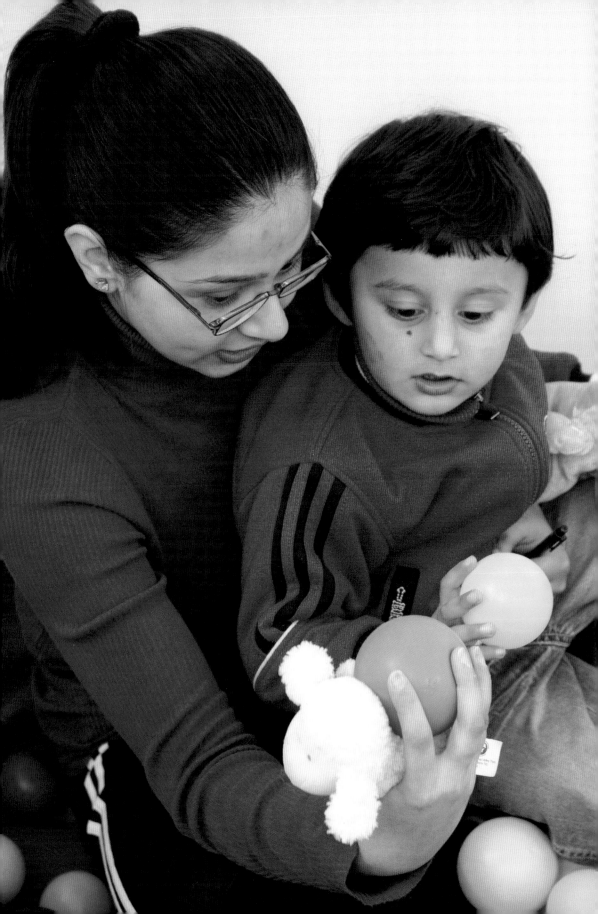

5 Respectful relationships

The Early Years Foundation Stage (EYFS) requires all children in settings to have a key person assigned to them who has a special responsibility for building respectful, trusting relationships with a particular group of children, getting to know them well as individuals, and making them feel confident and safe. The commitments also emphasise the need for that key person to work to establish a respectful relationship with each child's parents and family.

The research base in support of building respectful relationships with parents as the foundation for involvement is conclusive. Moran and others (2004) reviewed over 2,000 studies conducted since 1985 and summarised common findings. A key message is that relationships underpin all successful parental support programmes. Practitioners who build respectful relationships have more success in both attracting parents to engage and in maintaining their engagement over longer periods.

The Moran review concludes that parents respond well to confident, well-informed staff. They view practitioners as experts with valuable knowledge that they wish to benefit from. However, they like to have their own views and knowledge respected, and do not want simply to be told what to do: 'Recognising parents' expertise in their own children and lives, doing things with families rather than to them is crucial here' (Moran and others 2004, p.98)

The review also found that parents respond well to practitioners who show some understanding of the difficulties families face in their lives and who avoid making quick judgements or telling them that what they are already doing with their children is wrong.

Quinton (2004), reviewing key messages from research for the Department of Health between 1996 and 2002, and Tunstill and others (2005), evaluating the implementation of Sure Start, reach similar conclusions. Parents respond to sensitive, accessible individuals. They welcome professionally run services and expert advice, but they like these to be delivered in the context of more equal, friendly relationships. Parents want to be listened to and be seen as active participants in any problem solving. They have their own views and knowledge of their child and would like this be taken into account. Parents like to feel they have some control. In their everyday lives they are used to actively seeking solutions to the difficulties they face. They dislike feeling indebted to others and like to reciprocate the support offered to them. They want to keep this sense of control and reciprocation in their dealings with schools and services.

A group of parents at Coram Parents' Centre articulated similar views when asked what they valued most in those working with their families. In addition they said they liked practitioners who encouraged them, took time to get to know them and reminded them about the good things they did already for their children. They also expressed feelings of appreciation towards support workers who had 'gone the extra mile', been there in 'bad times', helped them 'calm down' and given them 'hope for the future'.

The main research findings, showing what parents want from a respectful relationship, are summarised in Research sheet 3.

Research sheet 3: What do parents want from a respectful relationship?

Practitioners who are:

- Confident and well informed.

- Approachable and reliable.

- Non-judgemental and understanding.

Practitioners who:

- Show interest in individual children and their families.

- View parents as experts on their own children and lives.

- Listen to parents and value what they already do to help children learn.

- Share a range of additional ideas and options to help learning.

- Encourage and build confidence.

- Include parents in decision making and problem solving in a more equal relationship.

Sources: Quinton (2004); Moran and others (2004); Tunstill and others (2005); and parents at Coram Parents' Centre.

Adapted from Resource sheet 3.2 PEAL Reader.

Practitioners capable of building this type of respectful relationship with parents are more effective in involving them in a child's learning and development. This requires practitioners who are prepared:

- To be open-minded, listen and get to know more about families

- To acknowledge a parent's right to active involvement in their child's learning within a more equal relationship – effectively a real learning partnership.

These two ideas often need considerable individual reflection, as well as discussion within teams. They form a major part of the PEAL training day when participants are asked to examine personal attitudes in a session called 'What might stop us?', and they are both considered at some length here.

Knowing more about families

Sometimes reluctance is expressed when 'getting to know more about families' is suggested as a way to increase parental involvement in early learning. Responses have included: 'This is being too intrusive in families' lives'; 'Families will view questions as unnecessary interference'; 'How parents choose to live is not our business'; and 'We need to keep a professional distance and not get emotionally involved'.

These concerns are understandable, but there is no intention that families should be faced with constant questions, grilling interviews and unwelcome intrusion, or that a practitioner acting as a key person should get deeply involved in families' lives. The Coram parents did appreciate workers who were prepared to 'go the extra mile' and give emotional support, and this clearly has a powerful impact on some parents' lives. Some practitioners will feel more able to support families in this way than others; and those working in an outreach/family support role will have more capacity to do so.

However, for effective everyday practice in settings, it is more a question of taking a genuine interest in family backgrounds and circumstances, developing warm relationships and adopting a sensitive approach to each individual family. What practitioners and settings need or want to know will vary according to each local community and each individual family, but information that might be valuable could include:

- parents' occupations/workplace and shift patterns

- who lives with the child

- significant extended family members

- who else cares for a child outside the home

- languages spoken at home

- countries of family origin and ethnicity

- immigration status

- family beliefs

- family attitudes to learning

- family interests.

It might be useful to establish some of this knowledge early on – at a home visit or during a settling-in period – while other information can be gathered gradually over time as a relationship develops.

How knowing more about a child's family helps involve parents in learning

Avoiding stereotypes and valuing difference

Knowing families well reduces the temptation to stereotype and make negative assumptions about parents' abilities, attitudes, lifestyles and interest in education. Siraj-Blatchford (2004) reminds us how crucial it is, when working with children, not to have low expectations because of stereotypes based on gender, class or ethnicity.

In the same way, we need to view parents as individuals and not assume that they share exact experiences, characteristics and views with others of their 'type' – whether this is based on gender, ethnicity, faith group, class, sexual orientation, age or disability. There is as much diversity within perceived 'groups' as between them.

Likewise, there are many different models of a family; for example, children may be cared for by one or two parents, members of the extended family, same sex parents or foster families. The more experience we have of getting to know individual people who make up families, talking to, home visiting and working with parents who have a different life experience to our own, the more we recognise and learn to value the differences.

Developing understanding and matching services to need

Families living in any one area are all very different from each other. They do not respond in the same way to a setting's efforts to engage. Therefore the more services and settings get to know individual families the more successful they are likely to be in engaging them; they can adapt approaches and strategies to meet the needs of families and offer a range of possible options for involvement (Whalley and the Pen Green Team 2001).

Knowing more about a family provides a greater understanding of the challenges it is facing. Being aware, for instance, that a family has an older disabled child or that a mother is working night shifts, may mean there is less tendency to make judgements about non-attendance at events, late arrival or apparent lack of participation in the setting generally. It may be possible to discuss other options for involvement, to offer some flexibility or make effective links with additional local support services as appropriate, based on individual family needs.

If family work and study patterns are known, as well as childcare needs and other commitments, the timing of any workshops, events, meetings and crèche facilities can be adjusted to maximise attendance. Knowledge about who lives in the family home and who else has regular care of a child means an approach to other regular carers and older siblings may be possible – and they may be able to engage in regular dialogue about a child's learning; they may also be encouraged to borrow and use equipment, read with children and attend events if parents are unavailable.

Hana's first language is Somali. She was very quiet in nursery. Her key worker had suggested that her mother spend some time in the setting with her, to help build her confidence. Her mother seemed reluctant, saying she really didn't have time because of her other children. However, she welcomed an additional home visit, where the key worker was able to meet Hana's father and older siblings. She learned that the family was under additional pressure, as one of the older children had special needs that required a lot of extra care. She listened to the parents' account of their own upbringing in Somalia, as well as chatting to them about Hana in nursery. Hana thoroughly enjoyed the visit! Establishing a relationship took time – but over the year, to the delight of Hana, her father was encouraged to come out on two local trips. Her brother was also able to come into nursery occasionally to read with her and chat to her key worker in the morning. Getting to know a little more about the family helped staff to understand the pressures they were facing, opened up more dialogue and benefited the child. (Source: PEAL practice example: *Keyworkers – Getting to know children and families*.)

Improving communication

A better knowledge and awareness of home languages spoken, translation and interpretation needs, and family literacy levels, enables adaptation of communication methods. This will mean more effective dialogue with families and is likely to elicit more response to requests to share information and observations on children. Some families may be happy to write, while others may prefer verbal feedback or the use of photographs.

Developing shared understandings about learning

Talking with parents, listening to their ideas, and finding out more about their own backgrounds and attitudes towards, plus experience of education, will all help in the process of trying to establish greater shared understandings about how children learn. This is important if the aim is to encourage parents to engage in more play and learning activities at home, complementing what happens in settings.

Parents may not, for example, share a belief and understanding of how children learn through play – choosing not to follow advice in the way they help their children learn at home. This is very common. Brooker (2002) studied children in a Reception class and found some Bangladeshi parents were particularly confused about school practice. They viewed play as something to be indulged, with no connection to learning. Children at home spent time joining in adult activities rather than playing. School was perceived as a place to work hard, not play. Other parents of children in the same class were also supplementing school with more formal learning at home.

Knowing what parents think about learning is important. If practitioners listen and positively acknowledge what parents are already doing at home to help their child learn, it opens up dialogue and makes offering other, additional or alternative options that much easier. In this example, the practitioners might affirm and reinforce how much children do learn as they work alongside parents at home, they might express their reservations about more formal workbook approaches while also accepting the parent's view that their child does enjoy and respond to this type of activity at home. They could also explain their own practice more fully, demonstrating how children learn through play and how adults can enable and engage in that play. Ideas for play at home could be offered and modelled for parents, and loans of equipment made. This acknowledges parents' own views, broadens parents' experience and offers them other options.

Extending learning already happening at home

Establishing some idea of the type of learning activities – both formal and informal – that are already taking place in a child's home also helps to make more effective connections between home and setting, because practitioners can pick up on children's interests and experience to extend learning. It may be that children cook regularly at home, help with gardening or cleaning, or have grandparents who take them out to local markets or places of worship. It would be possible, for instance, to invite grandparents to work in the nursery garden with the children or set up a market stall for role-play. This connects learning between the home and setting, providing continuity and helping a child make sense of their experience. It also supports parents in understanding that what they do at home on an everyday basis helps their child to learn. (See the story about Tia on page 39.)

Understanding children's conversation and behaviour

Knowing a little more about what happens at home also helps in the understanding and management of certain forms of child behaviour and response. Brooker (2002) found some Bangladeshi children disadvantaged because teachers were unaware of the differing expectations between home and school. Teachers valued active talking, participation and independence, whereas many of the Bangladeshi families encouraged passive listening when learning, and had not particularly developed or valued independence in their young children. Some children may be very quiet at story, circle or discussion times, or prefer working with close adult guidance, because they have learned this behaviour at home. Awareness of home practices like these might enable practitioners to think through strategies to enable such children to talk more at school. Teachers could also try to share their knowledge and work with parents, supporting them to see that encouraging greater independence might benefit their children at school.

Having a more complete picture of a child's life – perhaps recognising family names or knowing a little about a regular journey a child undertakes – also enables a practitioner to 'tune in' to a child's thoughts and talk about immediate events in a more meaningful way. This creates more informed, sustained conversation at higher levels to develop thinking, encouraging children to recall, make connections, speculate and reason. This is particularly useful for children who have speech and language needs or who are in the early stages of learning English as an additional language. Visiting children at home is an effective way to gain this level of familiarity and this point is illustrated by the following extract.

At nursery Pali, who is acquiring English as a second language, often speaks about members of his family, but staff find it hard to understand what he is saying. He also talks a lot about the number 8 and clearly recognises the numeral. By walking with him to his house, taking photographs and talking to his mother, his key person was able to find out the names of the people who live in his flat and understand their relationship to him. She also discovered that he lives on the 8th floor and likes to press the button himself for the lift. 'This my house (8), this my car (G – ground floor).' (Source: PEAL practice example: *Home visits.*)

Ways to get to know families

Ways in which effective settings get to know families and establish friendly relationships are illustrated in the following extracts from the PEAL *Reader* and PEAL practice examples. These highlight, in particular, the importance of establishing clear settling-in strategies and visiting families at home.

The extracts also include ideas for showing interest in and gathering information on family history, languages and traditions as well as attitudes to and experience of childcare, education and learning. Practitioners find that taking an interest in and knowing more about families is a far more stimulating and satisfying way of working. It gives the opportunity to learn and explore different approaches to and experiences of life within diverse communities. It broadens views so that practitioners realise there is more than one model of successful family life (Draper and Duffy 2006).

At Thomas Coram Children's Centre, Camden, all new families are invited to a meeting (in small groups) with their key worker and to visit the centre in action. All children also receive a home visit, where essential information is gathered about eating, sleeping, language development, comfort routines and people who are special to the child. Families can share their feelings about their child coming to nursery and they are asked if there is anything they would like staff to know about the family. All children have a settling-in period (one week for over threes, two for younger children) where parents may be needed to stay with their child. The whole induction process is seen as a time for staff and families to get to know each other.

As a child moves through the different age groups, key workers set up new introductory meetings for parents. Each year, one worker from each age group – babies, toddlers and kindergarten – moves so that at least one familiar face from the team remains with the child and its family. Parents know the key worker is their first point of contact, but also that they are welcome to approach any member of staff. Parents are able to build relationships with a range of practitioners.

"Knowing families well means less assumptions are made. We've found that you often think a parent must know about the importance of play and interaction with their child when, in fact, they may need support to realise this."

"We find that knowing parents well makes it easier to encourage them into workshops and other events."

(Source: PEAL practice example: *Key workers: Getting to know children and families.*)

Konstam Children's Centre, Camden asks parents to make an adult (family or friend) available for two weeks to help settle their child. During this period, parents are encouraged to spend time in the setting in order to get to know staff and each other, and see how children play and learn. The approach is flexible, with parents able to move away when their child seems ready, as long as they remain nearby and readily contactable. The centre takes this opportunity to discuss its aims and expectations for the child's care and learning. Parents help to prepare their own child's space, bringing in a few of the child's clothes, a changing basket and some family photos. Favoured objects are also welcomed so that the child has something familiar at nursery. Parents are asked to show and explain how they feed, change and comfort their child. Interpreters are organised so that parents can use their home language in these discussions. Practitioners also try to learn some key words and phrases in a child's home language.

An introductory meeting for new parents is also organised, where staff introduce themselves and talk about some of the procedures. Established parents then take new parents and families on short tours of the centre before sharing refreshments with them. This is followed by an open forum, without the staff present, so that new parents can chat to existing parents about anything they like, in a more open and relaxed way. (Source: PEAL practice example: *Settling-in – Getting to know children and families.*)

At the *Pen Green Centre for Under Fives, Northamptonshire,* key workers have always been called family workers to emphasise the importance of working with children and their families. Each family worker has up to 10 children in their group, and a base in an area of the nursery where they display their current interests and gather at group times. Family workers also hold family group meetings for the children and their families in their group. They come together, get to know each other and celebrate the children's learning. Family workers gather as much information as possible about the children. Children at the centre sometimes have complicated arrangements during the week, where they are looked after by different family members. Family workers have found that by asking the families to detail where their child is cared for during the week on a regular basis, they can be much more in tune with each child. (Source: PEAL practice example: *Key workers – Getting to know children and families.*)

The initial home visit, before the child begins nursery, is followed up with two or three additional visits each year during which workers, families and children get to know each other more closely and share information about the child's development. Parents often feel more relaxed and confident in their own home. This is particularly useful for parents who may lack confidence in attending group sessions or participating in other ways. Practitioners also gain from an increased knowledge and understanding of a child's home context. (Source: PEAL practice example: *Time to talk.*)

Teachers and nursery nurses at **Maples Children's Centre, Ealing** collected their own extended family photographs and displayed them on individual posters in the nursery entrance, with captions explaining their relationships and where people lived. Practitioners who are prepared to share some personal experience and information about themselves in this type of way often elicit a warm response. Families were invited to take home material – or provide their own – and display their family in the same way. This project took on a dynamic life of its own, with many fascinating posters produced representing the international nature of the school. Staff, families and children spent a long time reading, explaining the posters and asking questions. This highlighted the vast diversity – and similarities – in family patterns and experience, both between and within cultures, and generated many interesting debates and reflections.

Groups of parents made presentations about their home cultures in a series of 'International Parenting' workshops at **Coram Parents' Centre.** They focused particularly on experiences of pregnancy, child birth and child-rearing. Practitioners from the centre were invited to listen and found the presentations very interesting; it gave them a deeper understanding of different attitudes and experience of childcare. The material was published in a booklet, *Sharing our Stories.* (Source: PEAL *Reader.*)

More ideas to help form relationships and get to know families are considered later (in Sections 6 and 7). Additional information on the value of home visits is contained in Appendix 1 (PEAL practice example: *Home visits*).

Equal partnership

The second area for consideration is the idea of more equal relationships, with parents playing an active part in learning partnerships. This requires some reflection on what it means to work in partnership. Is there a useful model that helps in the context of children's learning and development?

Parents respond well when they are listened to, and have what they know about their child and what they already do valued. They prefer to feel active in the partnership, maintain control and make some choices. They respond best when they feel confident, and when expert advice is offered in the context of friendlier and more equal relationships.

Is it possible to work in a more equal way with parents? The word 'equal' often causes considerable debate in this context. It is true that practitioners and parents do not have the same or equal knowledge. Practitioners have studied, trained and can have a great deal of specialised knowledge and experience gained over many years, through working with a large number of different children and families.

However, it is important to acknowledge that parents know most about their own child. There can be more equality here in the sense that both parents and practitioners have equally valid sets of knowledge to contribute and equally important roles to play in a child's learning.

Pugh and De'Ath (1989) suggest this is more a question of 'equivalence'– practitioner and parent knowledge is not the same but it is equally important – while Easen, Kendall and Shaw (1992, at p.285) express the relationship between the two sets of knowledge as: 'The former constitutes a "public" (and generalised) form of "theory" about child development, whilst the latter represents a "personal theory" about the development of a particular child'.

When combined, in effective, regular, two-way exchange, the two sets of complementary knowledge and ideas benefit the child because individual learning needs and interests can be considered far more carefully; a whole picture of a child can be taken into account and learning can be planned more effectively in both setting and home.

Davis, Day and Bidmead (2002) suggest a partnership model based on the Parent Adviser approach. The PEAL team and trainers believe this is very helpful when thinking about and planning for greater parental involvement in learning.

The elements of the partnership model are:

- a common aim

- working together

- complementary expertise

- mutual respect

- open communication

- sharing power

- negotiation.

What does the partnership model look like in practice?

Parents and practitioners share the common aim of wanting children to learn. Parents are experts on their own child; they know a lot about what their children like, can do and what interests them. Parents know a child's history in detail and can help their child make connections from one experience to another – essential for the development of early thinking. They are the best source of information on their own disabled child or their child's special learning needs. They already do many things at home that help their children learn. If practitioners work together with parents, share regular observations, listen and tap into this expertise, combining it with their own knowledge and experience, then planning together for children's future learning will be more effective, both at home and in a setting.

Every week Tia goes to the market with her grandma. She takes the bus and helps her carry baskets home. Tia loves this outing, getting upset if she can't go. Finding out about this meant that her key person was able to set up market role-play in the setting, and find stories about shopping and markets to share and send home. She organised a local visit to a nearby market with some other families, taking photos that were displayed in the nursery. This work was shared with Tia's family – who sent in some baskets and material for the role-play corner.

In this way services and settings complement what parents are already doing. In order to facilitate this two-way flow of information and sharing of expertise, communication needs to be open, with parents aware that their ideas and initiatives are welcome. Practitioners can show respect for parents' views and listen actively, while giving clear information in return. Power, in terms of deciding on future action, is also shared more. Both partners can contribute ideas that they feel might help a child's learning and parents can take decisions based on a range of possible options to help and support at home, rather than being expected to simply do what a practitioner tells them. They can also have input into what is planned for their child in the setting.

In discussions, a practitioner can use expressions and questions that encourage participation, and give parents a chance to take action, select from options and initiate ideas:

"It sounds from what you say that she likes to ..."

"Do you think we should ...?"

"Would it help if ...?"

"Which game/book do you think she might like next?"

"How did this story/game bag go ...?"

"I thought she might enjoy this next ... or this ... what do you think?"

Parents can then actively select what they feel will work for them at home, fitting ideas into their existing routines. In this way, parents can feel more in control and are more likely to remain engaged in the process, as their ideas are listened to and valued.

Crucially, this also helps to build parents' self-confidence and self-belief as educators of their own children. In the Parent Adviser model of partnership, a practitioner aims to help parents feel good about what they are doing, and encourages them to take a lot of the credit for their child's success and achievement. This can go on to have an extended impact as parents remain involved, active and in control as their children grow older. They are more likely to feel confident in sustaining involvement and making their views known as their children move on through their education.

The PEAL *Reader* contains two diagrams that can be helpful in visualising this 'balanced', more 'equal' relationship between parent and practitioner. Figure 1 is an image of a pair of scales, suggested at one of the pilot training sessions (with thanks to Neena Chilton).

Figure 1

Balanced relationships

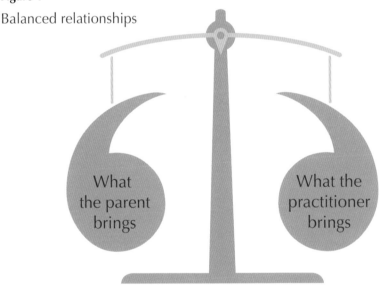

What the parent brings

What the practitioner brings

Source: Wheeler H and Connor J (2006), © Crown copyright

The partnership is not always equal – but one partner always complements the other. The scales tip and sometimes a parent provides the largest input to the dialogue, knowing more, giving more information, making suggestions; at others, a practitioner can have the greatest impact with an observation, idea or piece of knowledge that helps inform and enlighten.

Figure 2 also illustrates how the two partners complement each other and benefit the child through a continuing two-way flow of information.

Figure 2

Balanced relationships

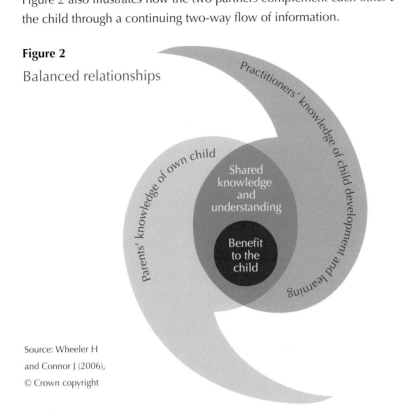

Source: Wheeler H
and Connor J (2006),
© Crown copyright

Davis, Day and Bidmead (2002) recognise that applying the Parent Adviser model is more demanding on practitioners. It requires very good communication skills, takes time and persistence to develop and, at times, means negotiation has to take place. However, working towards this model will lead to better outcomes for both children and parents because it matches what parents say works for them and what is known to be most effective in terms of maintaining engagement in the longer term. It encourages more involvement, generates more two-way communication about children's learning between practitioner and parent, and helps develop parents' own confidence – encouraging them to feel well equipped to help their own child, to create a strong home learning environment, take more control and make active decisions about their child's learning and education.

Knowing more about families and having a clear definition of partnership – which sets out the way a setting wishes to work with parents – helps to establish respectful parent–practitioner relationships. These relationships provide the underpinning foundation for practice in the most successful settings.

The next section looks in more detail at these successful settings. What additional steps do they take to involve parents as partners in learning?

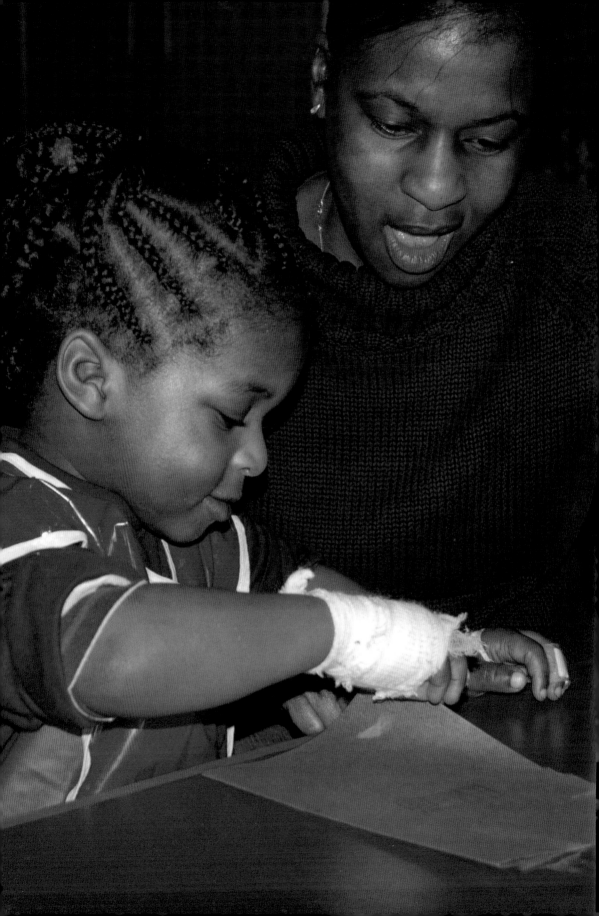

6 Involvement at the heart of practice

Commitment 2.2 of the Early Years Foundation Stage (EYFS) states that: 'When parents and practitioners work together in early years settings, the results have a positive impact on children's development and learning.'

Research supports this commitment. Settings and schools that achieve the best intellectual and social outcomes for children work closely with parents – they build parental involvement into the heart of their practice.

A summary of findings, showing how these most effective settings and schools communicate with parents is set out in Research sheet 4.

Research sheet 4: Effective settings and schools

The most effective settings and schools:

- Encourage high levels of parental engagement in their children's learning, work hard to build trust and help parents to see they have a role.

- Have staff with responsibility for parental involvement – establish clear strategies and evaluate impact.

- Share educational aims and practice with parents – and work to develop mutual understandings.

- Value information from parents and share information about individual children regularly (some on a monthly or even weekly basis).

- Encourage parents to be active in making decisions about their children's learning.

- Encourage parents to support children at home with activities and materials that complement those used in the setting.

- Work proactively to remove barriers to collaboration – making everyone feel welcome.

- Make efforts to know the wider community well and where other sources of support for families are located.

Sources: Siraj-Blatchford and others (2003); Desforges (2003); Sylva and others (2004); Siraj-Blatchford and Manni (2007).

Adapted from Resource sheet 6.3 PEAL Reader.

Many of the elements of successful practice highlighted here have already been discussed in earlier sections of this book. Effective settings understand barriers to involvement and try to overcome them. They recognise that the nature of relationships between practitioners and parents is critical. They work hard at establishing respect and trust, get to know families and adopt a model of partnership that values what parents say and encourages families to be active in making decisions. In this way, a major part of the professional role is seen as building parents' confidence as educators of their own children. These elements provide the foundation for success.

There are additional aspects of effective practice identified in the research that are given further consideration here. These are:

• Sharing regular two-way observations and supporting learning at home.

• Leadership, training and evaluation.

• Sharing educational aims and practice.

• Making everyone feel welcome – reaching out.

References are made throughout to PEAL materials and training where appropriate, and to key areas of debate that have arisen at PEAL training events. Section 6 concludes with a visual representation of all the principles and elements necessary to work successfully in partnership with parents – the PEAL model.

Sharing regular two-way observations and supporting learning at home

The EPPE study looked at settings that achieve excellent outcomes for young children, teasing out what aspects of practice were common. They found that these settings share child-related information between parents and staff regularly and that parents are often involved in decision making about their child's learning. Some settings hold regular monthly meetings with parents; with some even providing weekly feedback (Siraj-Blatchford and others 2003).

This level of communication requires practical steps that extend beyond newsletters or displays of information, termly parent evenings, open days or invitations to curriculum workshops. Although these are all valuable strategies, to be really effective parents need to be far more involved as individuals, exchanging very regular information with a key person about their child, and helping to plan for future learning.

This sounds very challenging. There are, however, some inspiring examples of practice contributed to PEAL from early years settings (see Section 7). They illustrate a variety of ways to share regular two-way observations and equipment with parents, complementing and extending learning between home and setting.

It is particularly hard to find the time and space for more regular two-way observations of learning in busy early years settings. This is the most commonly voiced reservation. Some ideas that have been found to work are set out on the following page (extracted from PEAL practice example: *Time to talk*).

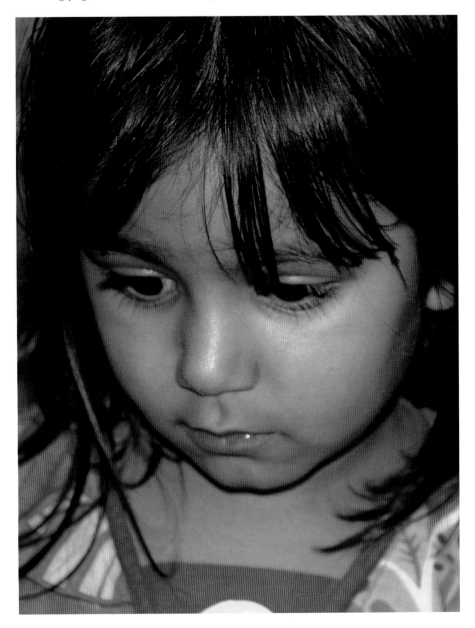

Coming and going

The time that children arrive and leave the nursery are the obvious points for parent contact, friendly greetings and farewells. This time can also be used to exchange information about learning and development.

Konstam Children's Centre, London Borough of Camden, always ensures that a member of staff is on the door to meet and welcome parents and children on entry. It is established that part of this role is to exchange messages between parents and key workers. The management team also has an 'open door' policy and parents are made welcome if they need to talk.

Thomas Coram Children's Centre, London Borough of Camden, has children arriving from 8am for an extended day, with many entering at 9.30am. Between 9.30 and 9.45am all key workers are available to prioritise talking with parents before any focus activities with children begin. It is established as a 'meet and greet' time. A senior member of staff is also available during the morning for parent consultations or to take a key worker's place if a conversation is urgent. Parents are aware that between 3.15 and 3.30pm is another good time to come in and talk, as children leave the setting. Parents of extended-day children are encouraged to arrive five minutes early, when possible, to allow for communication.

The Pen Green Centre for Under Fives, Northamptonshire, has a staggered entry. Families are able to arrive at the centre at any time between 8.15 and 9.45am. This means there is a steadier flow of families into the nursery so there is more time to converse, exchange information and learning observations with individual parents.

Extended parent consultation times and additional home visits

Extended consultations are held once a term at **Thomas Coram** to talk about progress, with parents, together. Children's needs and learning priorities are discussed. Thirty-minute sessions are made available for this during the nursery day. The time is extended for parents of children with special needs (up to an hour) so that Individual Education Plan review meetings can form part of the consultation with both the special educational needs coordinator and key worker in attendance. This means that parents don't have to make arrangements for two separate meetings, and practitioners benefit from the joint exchange of information.

Gamesley Early Excellence Centre, Derbyshire, has also extended the time and frequency of dialogue with parents. As well as two home visits, parents take part in at least three consultation meetings. These can last up to an hour and the time is negotiated to suit work and childcare commitments. A convenient time for families, plus persistent reminders, ensure full attendance. At each consultation, a record of achievement is shared and celebrated and a learning plan created based on a child's interests and needs. Activities that will be provided at school are talked through, and what the family can do at home to extend learning is also discussed. Parents borrow from a bank of equipment known as 'home school links' each week. Each pack has clear learning aims and objectives, which are discussed with parents, and then the child's response is shared upon its return. Visits out of nursery are also planned together at this consultation, so that parents can arrange to be free and accompany their child.

At **Pen Green** family workers can visit children and their families on a more regular basis. The initial home visit, before the child begins nursery, is followed up with two or three additional visits each year during which workers, families and children get to know each other more closely and share information about the child's development.

Leadership, training and evaluation

The most effective early years settings promote parental partnership as a central element of leadership practice. They are led by those who know their communities and staff well, work hard at establishing a collective team vision focused on children's outcomes, and encourage a collaborative, open approach where staff discuss and reflect on practice (Siraj-Blatchford and Manni 2007).

Effective settings are likely to have someone coordinating parental involvement or a specific post of responsibility. This nominee is often located within the senior management team and acts as a champion for the importance of the work throughout the setting. In this way all key persons, and anyone else working directly with families, can be encouraged to understand that talking with parents about children's learning, on a regular basis, is a major part of their role.

The coordinator can lead on the strategic implementation of ideas, including thinking through how to create more time to talk – for instance adapting staff rotas, organising cover or planning how space in the centre is used. They can ensure that evaluation and monitoring of impact takes place, including which parents are actually taking up opportunities to have home visits, to borrow material, attend workshops, volunteer and share observations. Is anyone missing out? They can also offer staff support and supervision in their work with parents and training needs can be prioritised. Lack of practitioner confidence in working with parents is one of the key barriers to involvement already identified in Section 4. It is possible to gain confidence and skills in working with parents from experience and practice and by learning from other colleagues. In-house sessions on parental involvement can be helpful and there are ideas in the PEAL *Training Guide* that can be adapted for use (see Section 9), but accessing specific training should also be considered. Training provides the opportunity for comparison of ideas and approaches, and more in-depth reflection. A list of training providers can be found in the 'Resources' section (page 118).

Sharing educational aims and practice

The EPPE research highlights the type of home-based activities that 'stretch a child's mind' and give children a particular advantage socially and cognitively as early as three years of age. These are activities that continue to be associated with achievement at later ages as children progress through school. They are discussed in Section 3 and recorded again at the top of Research sheet 5. The most effective settings share this type of research and information on child development and learning with parents, and support parents to provide stronger home learning environments, suggesting activities and loaning equipment to complement what happens in the setting.

They share other key aspects of child development and early years practice too, as indicated on Research sheet 5 – Also important for a child. Home-based play activities are best delivered in the context of warm, loving relationships that build a child's self-esteem. Children learn from active play and real experience, and should be allowed to follow individual interests, make choices, take the lead in play and have opportunities for sustained play. It is important to listen to children, extend their thinking with shared conversations, encourage their independence and (where their first language is not English) to maintain the use of a strong first language, while acquiring English as a second, both at home and in settings.

Research sheet 5: What activities create a strong home learning environment?

Activities that 'stretch a child's mind'

Reading with and to children	Singing songs and rhymes	Going on visits	Painting and drawing	Creating opportunities to play with friends	Going to the library	Playing with letters and numbers

Source: Sylva and others (2004).

Also important for a child

Research suggests that practitioners should share with parents the importance of the following.

Developing adult–child relationships that are loving, warm and responsive	Listening, responding, and vocalising/talking, from birth	Providing opportunities to learn in meaningful, enjoyable contexts	Recognising success, giving positive feedback – building confidence and self-esteem
Giving opportunities and encouragement to explore and develop independence – offering support when needed	Providing real experiences that make sense to children, including children in everyday routines	Following a child's interests, encouraging deep involvement	Learning through active play. Playing together, allowing a child to lead play
Listening to children; engaging in sustained, shared thinking – reasoning, speculating, describing, making connections and open questioning	Oral storytelling – and sharing stories at home about everyday life, past experiences etc.	Talking about words, letters and sounds in context – e.g. environmental print, picture books	Using a wide variety of text – encouraging repeating of favourite stories
Developing understanding of letter sounds and patterns	Encouraging and affirming early mark making and writing attempts	Knowing that growing up bilingual gives positive social and cognitive outcomes	Using and developing a strong first language whilst acquiring a second (including visual languages such as British Sign Language BSL)

Sources: Nutbrown and others (2005); Siraj-Blatchford and McCallum (2005); DfES (2002); National Literacy Trust (2001); Siraj-Blatchford and others (2002).

Adapted from Resource sheet 6.2 PEAL Reader.

Parents are entitled to know about research and educational practice – including what the EPPE team characterise as a strong early home learning environment. This sharing of knowledge and information should not, however, make parents feel that what they do already with their children is not valuable and productive. On the contrary, it is important to find out what learning activities already take place at home, build on them and enhance parent confidence. Plans for a child's learning are more effective if it is known, for instance, that a family tells stories rather than reads to children or encourages their child to work alongside them as they cook or work in the house. Home practices that may reflect elements of a family's culture or class should be respected, valued and reflected in a setting as much as possible. This helps a child make connections and make sense of their daily experience, and it builds confidence and gives continuity. It fits the model of partnership already discussed in Section 5 in which what happens at home is valued, reflected in planning in the setting, complemented and extended. In this way a family might be asked to share a traditional story or rhyme with a key person, or to come into a setting and cook with children – as well as being encouraged to benefit from additional options offered to share picture storybooks from a regular library loan or enjoy a home story visit with books, props and recordings. This approach is more effective as it values what is already happening, builds confidence and extends options.

The EPPE research has given rise to interesting debate and reflection at PEAL training events about how educational practice and understandings about learning are shared with parents. Some participants have commented that they feel the activities highlighted by EPPE, as indicative of a strong home learning environment, stress an emphasis on books and early literacy too soon. Some feel that this might make parents too anxious too early about school achievement, instead of relaxing, and enjoying play with their babies and young children. Others have said they would not feel comfortable in advocating them to some parents, especially those they know lack confidence in reading and writing, or those for whom English is not their first language.

A brief response to these concerns is outlined here and comes from a combination of thinking from the PEAL team, trainers and other participants sharing in the debate at events. First, books can be introduced to families in a range of sensitive and accessible ways. This might include for instance using books with one-line captions or no text, bringing books 'alive' with puppets and 3D props, using dual language texts and recordings, and making use of books with illustrative video, DVDs and story sacks. It is also possible to invite families in to hear stories with their children before sending a storybook home, make personal family books with photographs and simple text – and accompany families to the local library to help them enrol and feel comfortable in the library environment. Many of these ideas are illustrated in the extracts from practice examples in Sections 7 and 8 – such as 'Story home visits', 'Listening library', 'Home visits with story sacks' and 'Languages week'.

Home learning influences very early social and intellectual development – the impact isn't only on later school achievement. Children with strong home learning environments were found to have the ability to use language at higher levels, to concentrate, cooperate and feel more confident by the age of three. It certainly is important to relax, play and enjoy life with young children, but it is also important to know how to play in ways that stimulate thinking and develop social skills. The activities highlighted by EPPE include going on visits, making opportunities to play with friends, singing songs and rhymes, and drawing and painting. These emphasise sociability, creativity, and doing enjoyable things with others – as well as sharing books and noticing and playing with letters and numbers.

Although home learning is not just about books and early awareness of print, it is worth considering the potential power of books on very young children's development and advocating their use to families – and this should not be confused with current concerns and debates about pushing formal teaching of discrete literacy skills or phonics on young children. Talking to babies and young children while sharing picture books helps vocabulary, language and thinking skills develop – children can be encouraged to describe, recall experience, connect one idea to another, debate, reason and speculate on possibilities. Books also enable talk beyond the immediate, the here-and-now. Children and parents can enter a variety of other worlds together – real and imaginary – and discuss ideas and places of which neither have direct experience.

Children with a rich, interactive, early book experience also get interested in print at an earlier stage, noticing and talking about letters and writing in the environment, drawing and mark making, and becoming conscious of language as a symbolic system that carries meaning and can be 'played with' and acted upon. They turn to books for their own pleasure, often revisiting a text over and over again. Those who have been encouraged to join in with well known texts, to take over reading part of a story and 'play at reading' learn to read more easily at a later stage; they are likely to recognise some words on sight already and be able to predict the text (knowing what is likely to come next is an important skill for fluent reading).

It is beyond the scope of this discussion to explore the impact of early book sharing in greater depth, but useful starting points for more reading are:

- Whitehead, MR (2004) *Language and Literacy in the Early Years,* Chapter 7 'Books and the world of literature'. London: Sage Publications.

- Nutbrown, C (2006) *Threads of Thinking: Young Children Learning and the Role of Early Education,* Chapter 5 'Nourishing children's thinking through stories'. London: Sage Publications.

- Bookstart – a national programme that encourages parents to share and enjoy books with their children, from as early an age as possible (www.bookstart.co.uk).

Making everyone feel welcome – reaching out

Effective settings work hard at making everyone feel welcome. The Children's Plan recognises that much progress has been made in involving parents in learning in early years settings but that more needs to be done to reach out to all families. There has been interesting debate during PEAL training events about this, with some participants asking for special strategies to get families described as 'hard-to-reach' involved in children's learning.

Trainers have tried to encourage more reflection on the term 'hard-to-reach', and ultimately, rejection of it. As a phrase used in this context, it implies that families are very hard to interest in their children's education. There are, of course, some families living in very difficult circumstances who are harder to work with – particularly those who live with violence and/or addiction – where additional specialist support services and intervention are required. However, 'hard-to-reach' seems to have developed into a blanket term and is often used to describe families who might be seen to participate less – those from minority ethnic communities, single parents, young parents, and even fathers. It is often used to refer to families who do not join in and respond to what services offer. Perhaps they do not take up invitations to workshops, events or open evenings. They may, for instance, appear reluctant to spend time in a setting or appear in too much of a rush to talk about their child, not keep to rota systems to help, or they may be persuaded to sign up for, but then fail to continue with a series of family learning sessions.

Alternative phrases such as 'most excluded' families or even 'hard-to-reach services' have been suggested at PEAL events, to emphasise the fact that the onus is on services to reflect upon and adapt everyday practice in order to meet need. It is more valid to ask: Can services be made more reachable, more appealing, accessible and welcoming to all? One participant summarised this in her evaluation after a training day: 'It's not why parents are not attending; it's what we are not doing as a centre to enable them to participate.'

The reality is that services are often very hard for many families to locate, understand and reach. Some of the most disadvantaged families lack the confidence, knowledge, resources or time to access the opportunities on offer to get involved in learning. More of the barriers to engagement considered in Section 4 apply to them, often in complex combinations.

How do settings reduce barriers and reach out?

Effective settings consider what the major barriers are for their own communities and work proactively to remove them (Desforges 2003). This involves, as already established, forming relationships, knowing more about families, asking families what they need and offering a good range of options for involvement in learning that are matched to individual family circumstances (Whalley and the Pen Green team 2001).

Recognising that it may take a considerable time to reach out to some families is important. Participants at PEAL events have suggested that persistence is often needed, with practitioners who are aware that they need to avoid feelings of personal rejection. Some relate stories of gradually building confidence and relationships with families over a period of years.

"Everybody finds it difficult to deal with parents from time to time. But with support and time things can be resolved."

"I've learned all parents can be engaged given enough patience, support and time."

"I think it's our approach with parents that determines our success – some parents are difficult to engage but not impossible!"

Ensuring a genuinely friendly welcome to all on entrance – to both registered parents and those who may enter a building for the first time – is often highlighted in discussions. Making the physical environment more welcoming for parents is seen as essential too. If at all possible, providing a comfortable, relaxing space (or spaces) with adult furniture, where families can stay and talk to each other, make refreshments and allow younger children to play safely, pays huge dividends in terms of providing mutual support and relaxation.

Thinking through how to include all families is important; without this, some parents will be unintentionally excluded from participation. Parents may, for instance, avoid visits when financial contributions have been requested; be excluded because social occasions appeal only to certain parts of the community; or feel very uncomfortable about taking part if they feel they will be the 'only one' in a group – for instance, the only young parent, asylum seeker or father.

Particular attention may be needed to encourage fathers' involvement in early years settings. A summary of successful strategies is included in the accompanying box.

What gets fathers' involved?

- Positive attitudes, welcoming fathers personally.

- Targeting publicity directly at fathers and sending personal invitations by post.

- Children giving personal invitations to fathers.

- Consulting fathers – what would they like to do?

- Emphasising how a father's involvement will help a child's education.

- Inviting non-resident fathers to events and sending regular information to them.

- Short-term projects with fathers and children – such as ICT, outings, videos, sport.

- Asking fathers to help in practical ways that make use of their skills.

- Flexible timings that suit all work patterns.

- Holding specific fathers' groups or events.

- Ensuring displays and materials reflect images of fathers and young children.

* 'Fathers' denotes all those acting as a father figure.

Sources: Goldman (2005); Pre-school Learning Alliance (2005).

Practitioners need to have training in and show commitment to the setting's inclusion and equalities policies. Parents should feel confident that racism is not tolerated. The physical environment, personal attitudes, approach and practice all need to be considered in order to ensure that all parents see aspects of their lives reflected in the centre, and receive an equal welcome, space and time. Recruiting some staff from local communities and local parents themselves helping in outreach work have been found to be particularly effective in engaging minority ethnic families (Early Childhood Forum 2005; Page and Whiting 2007).

If workshops, classes or events for parents are offered, ensuring that care for younger children on site is arranged (or that younger siblings are welcome) is important, as is ensuring access for disabled parents and the provision of adequate translation and interpretation services. Local authorities may be able to offer assistance with the latter, but local community groups and parents themselves are a good potential source of support. Offering any workshops, consultations or events on a variety of days and at a variety of times will also help to maximise attendance, as will inviting parents face-to-face, not relying on written notices or leaflets.

It is also necessary to ensure that effective links are made, and direction given, to other services locally. Children's centres, working with local authorities, are making these links easier for families – for example to housing or benefits advice, and training or specialised support groups. Some centres will be fortunate enough to have additional services on site, or family workers who can make connections and support parents directly. At the very least, it is important for all settings to know where to access local services for families swiftly and efficiently. National organisations that can act as a starting point for information and additional support for practitioners and parents are listed in the 'Resources' section (page 118).

Home visits to talk about learning

The most effective strategy for inclusion of more families in early learning is home visiting. Parents often feel more relaxed at home and appreciate having time to talk on a one-to-one basis. This helps to develop relationships, builds confidence and encourages families to get more involved in learning activities at home. It can also be a useful starting point leading, as confidence grows, to more take-up of opportunities to engage in settings and with other services. Echoing the research on relationships in Section 5, the National Evaluation of Sure Start (2006) concludes that home visiting is more effective as a strategy when delivered by sensitive, persistent practitioners, capable of forming trusting relationships.

The evaluation also emphasises the importance of having more focus on children's learning and development in outreach programmes. Even when home visits were delivered by early education or special educational needs workers in Sure Start programmes, much of the time was often taken up on family support, especially helping mothers with depression or anxiety. The evaluation suggests there is a need for more long-term home visiting projects with the centre of attention on learning and development for very young children as well as family support, encouraging parents to feel enthused about their own child's potential to learn and achieve, even in the context of their own immediate difficulties.

Comments from participants at PEAL training when this issue has been discussed have included:

> "You do need to be sensitive and acknowledge the problems – but build in opportunities to talk about learning when you can too."

> "Some problems are ongoing and talking about the child and encouraging engagement in groups can help lift a parent out of depression and stress – it can help and be a positive experience."

> "I've found that sharing little observations about a child in a positive way is uplifting for some parents – it works as long as you have a good relationship with them."

Born to Learn – Coram Family

Coram Family's Born to Learn programme worked with parents of 1–3 year olds to support their child's learning and development. Family support workers provided a series of six home visits for families and held regular group sessions for parents to get together and discuss aspects of children's learning and development. They shared simple play activities with parents and left ideas for parents to continue with their children at home after a visit.

The team was trained in the Parents as First Teachers (PAFT) approach, which seeks to build parent confidence as educators of their children; and has also received Brief Encounters training, which supports practitioners to work with families experiencing common relationship problems. This training builds practitioner confidence and skills in active listening and in how to offer support using a simple counselling model.

At the end of the home visiting programme families reported reading and playing more with their children. The family support workers remarked on how many parents had gained in confidence and were more prepared to try new things. Talking with parents about their children's development proved to be an effective way to open conversations and develop relationships. Parents were encouraged to try joining in open drop-in and group sessions at the Parents' Centre.

You can read more about PAFT on page 88. Brief Encounters training is provided by One-plus-One (www.oneplusone.org.uk).

Additional information on the wider benefits of home visiting can be found in Appendix 1.

PEAL model

This section concludes with a visual representation of the principles and elements necessary to work successfully in partnership with parents – the PEAL model.

Figure 3

Parents, early years and learning model

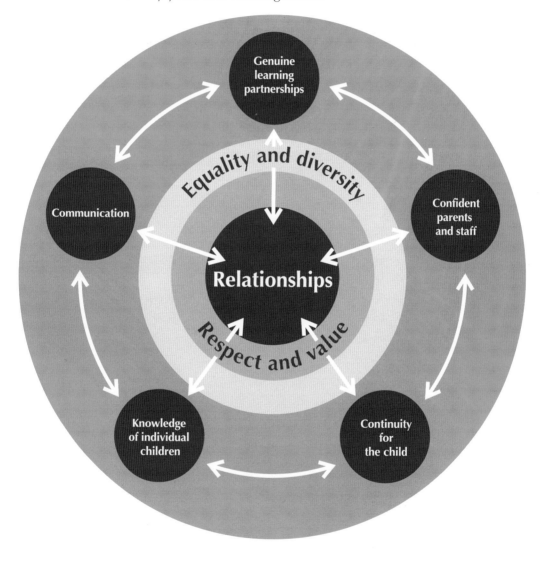

Source: Wheeler, H and Connor, J (2006), © Crown copyright

The model provides a simple illustration of the key elements that need to be in place to create genuine learning partnerships with parents in early learning. Relationships between parents, practitioners and children are at the heart of practice and provide the foundation. These relationships need to be built on respecting and valuing each other's contribution, and embedded in values of equality and diversity.

The three inner concentric circles need to be in place first to enable the surrounding elements to develop. In this way, parents and practitioners feel more confident and are able to communicate more effectively. Information flows backwards and forwards between settings and home, leading to greater knowledge of individual children. This provides greater continuity for children and more appropriate planning for future learning, based on children's everyday experience, individual needs and interests. Each element has an impact upon the others, and as the outer components develop, they serve to make relationships even stronger.

7 Practice examples

This section contains extracts from the original PEAL practice examples. These are given to all participants at a training event, and many can now be downloaded in full from the website. Additional examples of parent-partnership work are also included for the first time here, contributed by practitioners in children's centres who initiated or further developed projects after attending PEAL training.

The examples illustrate the many creative ways settings have found to put principles into practice and work more closely with parents – building relationships, exchanging two-way observations, taking learning into homes, lending books and equipment, and getting out and about with families.

As practitioners evaluate the impact of their parent-partnership projects, they say very similar things. There seems to be a common pattern of experience, and a clear process emerges in which practitioners notice that:

- knowledge of families and individual children increases

- practitioners become more understanding of parents' circumstances

- relationships with parents improve

- practitioners grow in confidence

- practitioners find their roles more exciting and interesting

- parents have more confidence in talking to practitioners

- parents develop their understanding of learning through active play

- parents recognise their child's achievements

- parents enjoy contributing to records themselves and helping to plan future learning

- children enjoy seeing their parents and key persons talking to each other.

The practice examples are grouped here under headings to provide some structure, but many actually relate to more than one category. The first set of practice examples illustrate a variety of ways to share observations and educational practice, include parents in planning for future learning, and provide activities and material for home learning. These are followed by examples focused more specifically on under threes; getting out and about with parents; taking learning directly into homes; involving fathers; and transition to primary school.

Sharing observations, knowledge and practice

Stop! Look! Listen! Sharing observations with parents

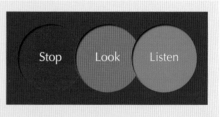

Camden's Early Years Foundation Stage Advisory Team has introduced the 'Stop, Look and Listen!' approach to a range of early years settings, to enable practitioners and parents to share their observations and plan the next steps for children together. The title suggests a way of working with young children, to be shared with parents, that encourages them to sometimes *stop* everything, *look* at their child as they play and *listen* to what they have to say.

The inspiration for the project stems from a combination of training on 'Listening to Young Children'* and the work of Margaret Carr in New Zealand on assessing children's learning through recording 'Learning Stories'.** Listening to Young Children suggests recording children's ideas as a vehicle for sharing experiences. Cameras, for example, can be used for a variety of purposes such as recording children's likes and dislikes; planning changes in the setting; and recording observations on walks. By using the format of Learning Stories (see Figure 4, page 61), parents in New Zealand's early childhood centres are encouraged to regularly observe their children, share their own children's interests and contribute to records. Parents and practitioners write an account of what children do and say when absorbed in play. These are then discussed and plans made to encourage positive learning dispositions, which are defined as: taking an interest; being deeply involved; showing persistence; expressing feelings and views; and taking responsibility.

Parents from a range of settings in Camden attended evening sessions where both approaches were explained by an advisory teacher. At the workshop, an example of a Learning Story was read out and it was explained that it could be very short – simply recording what a child did and said. Both practitioner and parent use the same recording format. Some parents agreed to make observations of their child at regular intervals. Some managed each week, others every half term. The child's key person also makes an observation and these are shared. Parents do express anxieties about involvement at first, feeling uncertain of what to say or write but they are encouraged to think about what interests their child, what gets them involved, and to observe this. The observations can be written down, taped, videoed or, for those who feel uncomfortable about writing, simply recounted verbally. Disposable and digital cameras have also been given or lent to families to help recording, and have proved very popular.

Through this process, parents learn new things about their children. They notice what really interests them, spot repeated behaviour patterns, realise that children can do far more than they thought and even begin to consider that perhaps they had been pressurising them to do things they did not like. Through relating observations to Margaret Carr's Learning Stories, parents are supported in appreciating the prime importance

> I didn't realise he could do so much for himself. I've stopped doing everything for him now, the way I used to.

of personal, social and emotional development in learning. They also realise just how much children learn through play and how important it is to give children time to explore and lead, instead of adults dictating the pace.

*Lancaster and Broadbent (2003); www.coram.org.uk **Carr (2001); www.communityinsight.co.uk

Figure 4

Learning Story assessment format

		A Learning Story
Belonging	Taking an interest	
Well-being	Being involved	
Exploration	Persisting with difficulty, engaging with challenge	
Communication	Expressing ideas or feelings	
Contribution	Taking responsibility	

The Learning Story assessment format can be downloaded at www.peal.org.uk
Source: Carr (2001)

Sharing observations with parents: The Pen Green Loop

All parents at the **Pen Green Centre for Under Fives, Northamptonshire**, are encouraged and supported to feel confident about their involvement in their child's learning. The Pen Green Loop is a model developed to maximise the dialogue between parents and nursery staff about learning. It provides for a continuous two-way flow of information from nursery to home and from home to nursery. The loop shows the child at the centre.

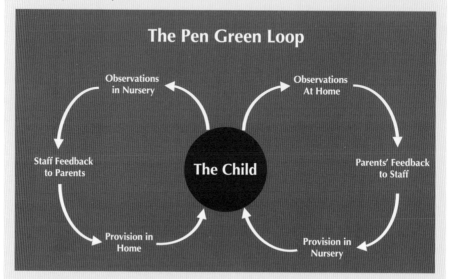

Parents are asked to share observations of their children at home, regularly. These can be communicated verbally or via a written diary, photographs or video clips. These observations are fed into family worker and team planning, so that future activities can be based on an individual child's interests and

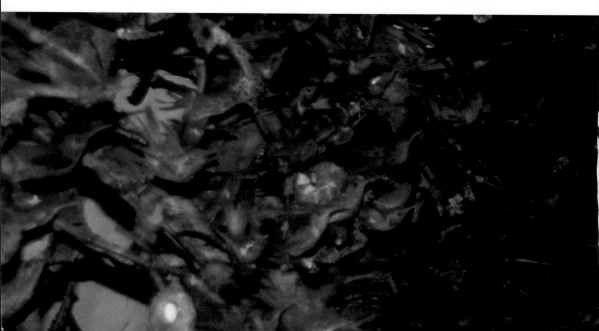

patterns of behaviour and thereby enhance learning. Observations made at the nursery are shared with parents regularly, which in turn can affect provision at home. Parents and practitioners work in partnership to extend the children's learning in a meaningful and enjoyable way.

Parents are offered a wide range of opportunities to become more involved. They are invited to attend sessions in which staff share their knowledge and theories of child development. Parents can continue to attend regular study sessions to discuss their child's ongoing development. These sessions are provided at various times of the day to suit working and family patterns. The key concepts they focus on are: well-being (Laevers 1997), the importance of emotional well-being and the impact this has on learning; involvement (Laevers 1997), how to recognise learning when children are deeply involved; schemas (Athey 1990), for use in recognising and planning for repeated patterns of behaviour; and pedagogic strategies (Whalley and Arnold 1997), how to interact sensitively and effectively with children. Videos of children playing at nursery are shown to parents and these give a shared focus and stimulus for discussion. Parents are strongly drawn to these videos as they are interested in watching their own child, and in talking about their learning and the interesting things that they do. Showing the videos at evening meetings has been particularly effective in attracting fathers, who are invited through personal invitations to discuss their own child. Nursery staff create opportunities for parents to initiate and sustain an ongoing, open dialogue. Parents needing more support are offered one-to-one discussions. More information on the training available at Pen Green can be found in the 'Resources' section, page 118 (and at www.pengreen.org).

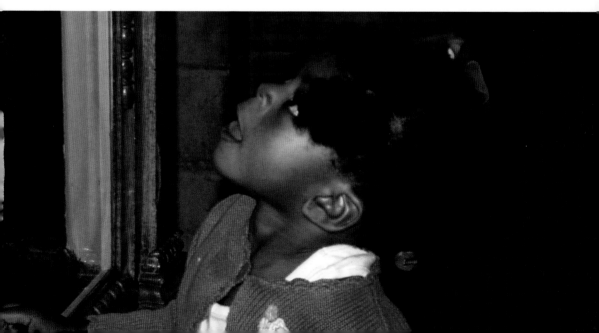

Sharing records with parents

At **Thomas Coram Children's Centre** parents receive regular written reports on their children's learning and development, but these are complemented by ongoing 'easy to access' portfolios. These large display books provide an attractive visual record of a child's time in the setting.

These books include observations, drawings, paintings, early writing, photographs, and written narratives of children's play and talk. In this way, a child's progress is made very clear and can be celebrated by child, parent and practitioner alike. Other settings have developed similar 'record of achievement' boxes or books. This type of record keeping can be kept out in the main nursery area, easily accessible, so that parents and children can look through the record at any time. They can be annotated with comments in which practitioners explain the learning significance of what the child has achieved or said. References to the Early Years Foundation Stage can be made as appropriate.

Children take great delight in sharing their records, with other children, their families and practitioners. They become active participants in gathering examples of work and discussing with practitioners which items to include. Children can be encouraged to look back, reflect and recall just how much they have changed and learned over time. The portfolio becomes a real source of pride, helping to build self-esteem and confidence. The portfolios/boxes can be taken home to share with extended family. Parents can be actively encouraged to contribute valuable information to records. Using both parent and practitioner knowledge in this way, gives a more complete picture of the child, producing a more in-depth and meaningful record of their individual strengths and progress. Plans for future learning activities can then be matched more effectively to a child's interests and abilities.

❝❝ She loves looking through it at home. She tells me what all the pages say, over and over again. ❞❞

Sharing Treasureboxes® with parents

At **York Rise Nursery, London Borough of Camden**, practitioners received training on Treasureboxes provided by Linda Thornton and Pat Brunton of alc associates ltd. Treasureboxes are collections of themed resources chosen to engage children's attention, encourage their curiosity and spark their imagination. They provide starting points for investigation and exploration of the world and build on young children's ideas and understanding. It was decided to adapt this idea and share learning aims and observations with parents.

The nursery chose the theme of light to explore with the children. Practitioners developed four 'take home' boxes, using plastic toolboxes from a hardware store, so that children could borrow a selection of equipment for use at home. Children, parents and key workers chose from a range of items already used in nursery, such as a light box, torches, coloured transparent paper and reflective materials. Children in each key worker group took turns to take a box home and keep it for four days. A card was enclosed, with a list of ideas on how to use the equipment and possible questions to consider together. Disposable cameras and pads of sticky notes were also provided in the boxes so that parents, if they wished, could record what children said and did with the equipment. These photos and observations were brought into nursery to share with key workers. Parents had a variety of ways of communicating – some wrote observations, some took photos, while others preferred just to talk about what had happened.

Additional play boxes were then made for children to borrow – for sewing at home, and exploring the themes of animals and dinosaurs. In this way children consolidate and extend their learning through repeating, at home, the actions and vocabulary they explored at nursery. Children who usually have no 'product' to take home can feel proud of their boxes and develop confidence and self-esteem as they explain to parents what they know and can do. Parents' observations on their children from home are included in their records of achievement and this shared knowledge is used to plan for future learning.

Training on the use of Treasureboxes® is provided by alc associates ltd (www.alcassociates.co.uk or e-mail info@alcassociates.co.uk). Treasureboxes® is a registered trademark of alc associates ltd, covering publications, training and resources.

Drama and movement through stories and music

Collingham Gardens Nursery, Coram Fields Nursery and Holly Lodge Playgroup in Camden worked with their Foundation Stage Advisory Teacher to involve parents in their children's learning, by using drama and movement in stories and music. Music and movement sessions were held for parents, practitioners and children, led by Anni McTavish,* an early years creative arts trainer. She took everyone on an imaginary journey using a puppet, story and music. Some parents felt a little reluctant to participate at first, but gradually relaxed and joined in acting, singing and dancing with ribbons and simple props. Some practitioners also had to overcome their own feelings of awkwardness, developing their confidence to 'perform' with parents in the room.

Large cloth bags were then made, which contain a puppet, music book, CD, and a collection of coloured ribbons and bright silk cloths for dancing. A number were made in each setting with some available for parents to borrow. Now everyone in the family can continue to move and travel on imaginary music and story journeys at home. The bags encourage open-ended play so that children's imaginations can take them anywhere. Disposable cameras have been added to the bags so that parents can record their child's experiences, and then share them with practitioners. The nurseries use digital cameras so that practitioners can, likewise, share their observations of the children with parents. In this way, a flow of discussion about the child can take place between parents and nursery.

Inviting parents in to join any regular singing, dancing and story session enables parents to gain a sense of their child's enjoyment and gives an opportunity for practitioners to share what is known about how children learn from this type of experience.

*A sample session written by Anni McTavish is available on the PEAL website (and she can be contacted at annimctavish@tiscali.co.uk). A copy of her book, *Sing a Song, Tell a Tale: Enriching Children's Experience Through Music, Drama and Movement*, is available from Early Education (www.early-education.org.uk).

Adventures in play

A range of early years services and providers in **Norfolk** combine to share with parents the educational value of role-play. They organise a workshop to take place over two days: on the Friday, the children attend with nursery practitioners; and on the Saturday children attend with their families. Role-play scenarios are set up, indoors and out, for families to play together. These include, for example, a garden centre; health centre; dog show; 'Three Bears' cottage; building site; jungle; and journeys such as 'under the sea', 'to the moon' or a paradise island. Children and parents can take part in a pretend wedding, washing day, driving test or explore a Traveller's trailer. Practitioners are available on the day to take part and talk to parents about the value of imaginative play. Parents are able to see their child having fun, observe children totally involved and absorbed in play, and think about how this helps learning. By taking part, parents become more aware that involving children in everyday activities, such as shopping or washing, will help their learning. Norfolk Children's Services have made a series of role-play boxes for settings to borrow and hold their own sessions for parents.

❝ I was amazed at what they were doing in the baby clinic. I never realised my daughter knew so much about looking after babies. I could see how much she was learning. I have learned how important it is to involve her in the things I do at home. Perhaps I can persuade my husband to let her help him clean the car! ❞

❝ It made me realise it is not necessary to have expensive equipment, but I can use things I have at home already. ❞

Sharing observations with video

At **Beeches Pre-school, Peterborough**, video footage is taken of children playing in session. This is then shown to parents in a series of workshops, in order to support and share an understanding of learning through play. Families are offered regular weekly workshops, timed for the start of each part-time session (9am and again at 12.15pm). The workshops focus on different areas of learning and include play, early writing, early numeracy, speaking and listening, and using books with children. Video footage, shot each week ready for the workshop, focuses on the particular area of learning to be discussed. Parents are attracted into the session because they are interested in seeing their own children on the video.

The sessions are very short, just 20 to 30 minutes, so that busy parents do not have to give up too much time. Younger siblings are welcome to come along. An interpreter for the main community language is provided. Inexpensive activities are suggested, for continuation at home, and the ideas are repeated in handouts given out at the end of the session. Free 'mark making' packs are also made available to take home as an added incentive. These contain simple, attractive writing implements, notepads and paper supplies for children. The preschool has no computer but uses two digital video recorders connected to a television via a plug-in cable. Film can then be played back immediately and easily. The cameras are lent out to families so that parents can show children playing at home, and can share special occasions such as weddings, birthdays and holidays.

> ❝ Using video of children playing helps to 'break the ice' in parent workshops. Parents love to see their own children on screen. ❞

Family maths games library

At **South Acton Children's Centre, Ealing**, the maths games library contains games, toys and equipment for children and parents to explore colour, shape, sorting, number, pattern and measuring. Most game bags are built around story or information books that relate to the concept. All parents have an induction session where the importance of taking a relaxed attitude and enjoying the time with their child is emphasised. They are encouraged to follow their child's interests and allow the child to lead the play. Each bag has a laminated card with content details and ideas of how to play with the equipment. Some parents are involved in helping to maintain and lend out the games

and parents have helped to translate the instructions into community languages. Key workers follow children's development and make recommendations for which games to borrow next.

Parents are asked for their comments on the games and their child's response. These can be written down, but exchanging observations verbally, when the game is returned, works best. Parents are also invited to attend a series of workshops on how to develop their child's thinking and interest, but using the library is not dependent upon this. All children are enrolled and take-up is monitored very closely, so that families who have not borrowed are encouraged to do so. A curriculum booklet, *How to Help Your Children with Maths*, has been published to accompany the library. This has also been translated into the two most common community languages.

The storybook *Ten in a Bed* is provided along with suggestions for singing and acting out the rhyme with fingers or soft toys on a bed. Cards with numbers and signs on them are also enclosed to encourage numeral recognition.

> ❞ *I am more patient when I play with her. I follow the instructions on the card that break the games down into steps, so I don't rush her now.* ❞

Listening library

Gamesley Early Excellence Centre, Derbyshire, operates a regular 'Listening Library' for children and families. The aim of the scheme is to enable children to access and listen to 'core stories' in the home setting. Many of the children in the setting are not read to or told stories on a regular basis at home. Some parents may find this difficult, for a variety of reasons. The Listening Library contains packs comprising a bag, a copy of a core book, cassette player, and a cassette with a story recorded by a member of staff. Before beginning to borrow from the library, children are taught how to operate the cassette player so that they can use the equipment as independently as possible. The scheme helps to develop confidence within the children, allowing them to make independent decisions on when to listen to a story. It also enables them to listen to the same story over and over again. A video and DVD collection is now being developed to complement the existing stories on cassette and help build parents' own confidence in reading stories to children and developing the 'art' of story-telling. The video/DVD library packs comprise a video or DVD, a core storybook and book bag. Members of the centre staff have been videoed reading one of the core stories. It is very special for a child to see a significant adult from their nursery setting on the television at home!

Initially the story is read through once – using a variety of voices, intonation, facial expressions and gestures. This modelling of how to read a story is felt to help illustrate to parents the ways in which a story can be read to best effect. The story is then read through a second time, with the adult stopping to ask questions and make comments based on the pictures or text. Again it is felt that this empowers parents and builds confidence to move on to reading to their children in a way that encourages interaction between adult and child. When the family returns the cassette, video or DVD, the children are encouraged to retell the story to a member of staff. This is recorded, typed up on the computer, printed out and shared with the parent.

The centre is also beginning to adapt this approach for the very youngest children too. Packs will include a nursery rhyme tape, CD, video or DVD. The recordings will be made of children from the setting singing familiar nursery rhymes and songs. A rhyme book has already been produced to accompany the packs.

Toy library

Selby North Children's Centre, North Yorkshire, has set up a Toy Library with around 70 items that support all areas of learning and development. The books, toys and games encourage parents to have fun with their children and help them learn. Parents and children can browse toys and

> *I know what she'll be doing when she comes home! It encourages them doesn't it?*

resources in the setting and choose one to take home. A simple tracking system allows staff to 'check-out' and 'check-in' the resources as they are borrowed and returned. At the same time, parents and carers have an opportunity to talk to staff about their child's learning and next steps.

The setting has invited the Home-School Support Worker to join the project. This 'joined-up working' with staff from the primary school is proving invaluable. The support worker has given time to focus on building relationships with parents. She introduces herself over coffee/refreshments and supports less confident parents to choose and borrow resources. In this way the setting is able to focus on families it is felt would benefit from additional support and encouragement. Parents are extremely positive about the library. The children have also been very excited when talking about the games and books they have taken home. Over half of all families in the Foundation Stage use the library on a regular basis. Parents and staff are talking more and parents are playing a much greater role in planning their children's learning. Parents have also been observed talking *with* their child and *about* learning more often. The centre staff are extremely pleased with how the project is going and feel it is making a positive contribution to the home learning environment for many of their children.

Activity boxes

The Dove Children's Centre in Wolverhampton has developed activity boxes that parents can share with their children at home. Each box has a focus, such as healthy eating or musical instruments. The boxes come complete with clear directions for use and a notebook so that parents and practitioners can exchange comments about children's learning. Families can borrow a box for up to two weeks.

The boxes help to promote the importance of parents playing and interacting with their children as part of everyday life. Parents are encouraged to listen and observe their children as they play and note what they have said and experienced. This information is then shared with the child's key worker on a one-to-one basis. Parent and practitioner discuss what went well, what could be developed and any further ideas for activities in order to move the child's learning forward. Information gathered from parents is also included in the child's development profile.

Parents have been actively involved in the design and construction of the boxes. They have helped to think through ideas, ordered equipment, discussed how the boxes might be used and tested out their new found skills. Parents have shared ideas with each other, talked more about what their children enjoy doing and informed practitioners of what they do at home to extend learning. Involving parents in this way has allowed parents to take ownership of the project. It has developed skills and increased confidence and self-esteem. It has also given parents more insight into what play activities are possible at home, and just how much children learn through enjoyable play.

Languages week

At Thomas Coram Children's Centre, London Borough of Camden, one week in the year is designated as Languages Week in order to celebrate the varied home languages spoken by children and families in the community. Over 50 per cent of children speak a language other than English at home. Hearing their home language spoken and valued in the centre promotes a child's self-esteem and sense of security. The week helps everyone – parents, practitioners and children – to gain more understanding about language development and about different languages and cultures. Parents who are uncertain of the importance of maintaining a strong first language, while acquiring English as a second language, are reassured that speaking, playing and reading to children in their home language is the right thing to do.

Languages Week is promoted through the regular newsletter, by key workers inviting parents personally, and via a display showing activities from previous years. A workshop for parents is also run to encourage participation. Parents are invited into the centre to take part in activities – to cook, talk and play, read stories or sing songs and rhymes using their home languages. The school library service and a local bookshop are invited to bring resources into the centre. Parents can then look at a display of books appropriate for young children, including dual language texts, and have the chance to discuss the importance of reading regularly. Books are available for purchase. Evaluation shows that 59 per cent of parents have been encouraged to participate in Languages Week. The event has been successful in encouraging fathers' participation. The success might be due to all the staff heavily promoting and planning the week. The fact that parents could participate in a wide range of activities, choosing something that they felt most comfortable with, might also be a factor.

Peers Early Education Partnership (PEEP)

Sure Start Battersea runs PEEP sessions every week. Parents and children meet in age-specific groups – babies, ones, twos and 'pre-nursery'. Parents are able to socialise and support each other as well as play with their children, sing, read stories, and discuss issues concerning early learning and development with a range of early years and health professionals. The groups are led by a teacher and have input from health visitors, dieticians, and speech and language therapists, who have all received PEEP training.

The sessions start with a 'welcome time', when parents and children are encouraged to settle in and feel comfortable. This is followed by singing the Hello song in a circle, greeting each child by name. Parents and children join in with more songs and action rhymes and then share a mixture of stories and play activities together, usually planned around a particular theme. Parents also have a chance to discuss a particular aspect of child development.

In Sure Start Battersea, parents share new steps for their child in what has become known as the 'check-in' session. Parents can take it in turns to update the group on their child's progress and discuss their own experience of parenting, giving and receiving support from each other. Parents are given ideas to use at home with their children and picture storybooks can be borrowed to share. All families have a PEEP song book, plus CD-ROM, so that songs and rhymes can be practised at home. These are particularly popular. PEEP Learning Together folders are made available during the sessions for parents to use and borrow. The videos are also used in some of the groups and can be borrowed for home viewing. Some parents are reluctant to join in groups at first and, at

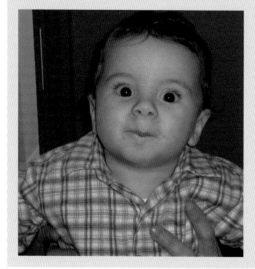

their first PEEP session, appreciate the company of a family support worker who is already known to them through outreach work. This initial support can help to build trust and enable the inclusion of all families.

More information on PEEP and PEEP training can be found in the 'Resources' section, page 118 (and at www.peep.org.uk).

Sharing ideas for play and observations: Childminders

Julie, a childminder in Barking and Dagenham, regularly shares with parents ideas about how play activities help learning and development. She invites parents to spend a little time at her home, joining in an activity with their child. Julie also uses a digital camera and prints out pictures of the children involved in activities during the day to show parents when they collect their children. These offer great talking points and opportunities to share moments together that cause particular delight and interest.

Childminders keep records of learning in all sorts of ways and each observation, exchanged with parents, helps to build a shared understanding of individual children. Julie keeps a book with a page for each child. She records the highlights of the day and shares these with parents when they come to collect their child. Parents can then follow on the activities at home or talk about them with their child. Julie encourages her parents to write in the book so that she can also refer to activities the children have done away from her setting.

Karen, a childminder in South Gloucestershire, invites parents to bring in items – books, toys or games – to support topics she is exploring. Whatever a child has shown a particular interest in, is discussed with parents at pick-up time and encouragement is given to continue the discussion at home, or on the journey home. Karen also produces newsletters in order to share current themes. She describes activities and outings she is planning to help children learn and explains how these link to the EYFS. Each child has a scrapbook of pictures showing what they have done at Karen's home or in the garden and on local trips. The book is shared with parents and copies of favourite photos are sent home. Parents can then talk with their children, prompting them to remember events. Karen also keeps a diary of each child's progress, matching learning to the EYFS. Sharing this regularly with parents helps them to engage with what she is doing with their child and to extend learning at home.

Dawn, a childminder in Barking and Dagenham, uses a karaoke box to encourage her children to sing rhymes and songs. These recordings are shared with the parents. She keeps a record of planning on the inside of a cupboard door – and observations on post-it notes. This provides a quick and easy way to tell parents about their child's achievements.

The National Childminding Association offers advice, networks, training and quality improvement schemes for childminders (www.ncma.org.uk).

Under threes

Toy library and treasure baskets

Wellholme Park Children's Centre, Calderdale, has a toy and book library that is open and accessible to parents at any time and all members of staff take an interest in helping parents make their selections. Sometimes a suggestion is made to a parent to take an item or book from the library that their child has shown a particular interest in during the week, thereby extending the learning directly into the child's home.

Treasure baskets are used regularly in the setting with babies and young children. These baskets are filled with a selection of natural or everyday objects such as fir cones, large pebbles, sponges, wooden and metal utensils, ribbon, whisks, balls and so on. Open-ended play provided by treasure baskets can sustain children's attention and thinking for much longer than a commercial toy that may only have one purpose.

In order to share the educational aims of the baskets with families the staff team decided to loan some out to parents as part of the regular toy library service. A simple leaflet was prepared to accompany the baskets, giving examples of objects that could go into a treasure basket and information on how a child's senses are used as they explore. The response has been very positive, enabling parents to see that baskets of everyday objects are a great way of engaging young children in learning using all their senses. Parents have come to appreciate more that babies and young children learn by testing everything they encounter in everyday life. It has helped parents to see that learning does not just happen when there is an 'end product' of some kind to take home at the end of the day – and some parents have created their own treasure baskets at home. (See Roberts and Featherstone 2002; and Hughes 2006.)

❝ One parent put together a treasure basket for her 11-month-old baby. She collected different brushes from around her house, an idea she had picked up from nursery. She was astonished at how long her baby spent playing with and exploring the basket. ❞

Home-Nursery diaries 0–2s

Wellholme Park Children's Centre, Calderdale, has developed and introduced a Home–Nursery diary system that has proved very beneficial to the two-way communication necessary to building up strong relationships between parents and staff. The diary is an attractively presented, A5 ring binder file, with

the child's photograph on the front. The diary pages have the key worker's input on one side with details about the child's day in the nursery. The information includes the food and drinks the child has had, sleeping times, nappy changes and activities they have shown an interest in and enjoyed. In addition, there are details about the child's general well-being, which may include notes on whether they have been happy and settled, discontented or ill in any way. This information can be shared verbally with parents but it can, most importantly, go home with them at the end of the day.

Once parents get the opportunity to look at the diary, they can complete the parent feedback section, if they wish. The reverse of each page has space for parents to fill in any comments they would like to make in return, or their own observations from home, such as on health or care issues, vocalisations and words spoken, preferred music and songs. Some parents have included photos of outings they have been on, which are welcomed. It is made clear to parents that there is no pressure for them to record anything. Parents return the diary to the centre when their child next attends. The diary is read by the key worker who follows up any queries and comments, or notes any particular needs and interests the child might have. The diaries are then kept in accessible boxes in the nursery, for convenience in terms of updating, or referring to them for information.

Baby and Me: Using DVD to share knowledge with parents

Sure Start Church Street, Westminster, provides a service for families from a wide range of cultural, ethnic and religious backgrounds. The main languages spoken in the area are Arabic, English and Sylheti. The team is made up of a variety of health and other professionals who work closely with local agencies, pooling knowledge and resources to meet families' needs effectively. The team works to build parents' confidence and understanding of how best to interact with their child. The team wanted to reinforce the message to parents that *they* are their child's first teachers, that communication skills start at birth, and that they are the people who can make a real difference to their children. Getting it right at the beginning has long-lasting effects. Sometimes parents are not aware of the different abilities of very young babies. This can lead to even less interaction where a child has special needs. It is estimated that 25 per cent of all new mothers in Westminster experience post-natal depression. At times, fathers can also display signs of depression. This can lead to less talk and interaction with babies, which can, in turn, lead to difficulties with communication skills in later years.

The early weeks and months are a good time to support parents' communication and interaction with their babies. Sure Start Church Street decided that using film would be most useful. They worked with local families and made a DVD, which shows parents and carers being the experts: talking with, playing and soothing their babies. Simple tips are given on how to tune in to a baby – consoling, touching, talking, listening, copying a baby's vocalisations, waiting for a response and turn taking, following a baby's lead, naming things of interest, using the home language, singing and playing. Simple explanations of how this helps to build brain connections to enhance the development of language and a healthy emotional bond are given, alongside delightful footage of babies and parents interacting. Parents are encouraged to have fun and give it a go. The DVD is used in a variety of groups – in baby clinics, ante-natal classes, post-natal wards, and on a one-to-one basis with families on home visits.

The *Baby and Me* DVD (2007) is available from The Children's Project (0845 094 5494; info@socialbaby.com) and is produced in either Arabic, English and Sylheti, or Polish, English and Portuguese.

Baby and toddler groups

 Setting up open access 'stay and play' sessions for parents, babies and toddlers is one way to begin sharing messages about learning and development, and build parents' confidence as educators of their own children, from their very earliest days. *St Anne's Stay and Play Group, Colchester*, meets twice a week between 10am and noon during term times, and on some mornings during the holidays when older siblings are also welcome to attend.

At every session there is a focus activity, such as collage or messy play. Helen Fraser, who runs the group, and her helpers encourage participation and explain the purpose of the play to parents. There is, of course, no pressure to join in. If children are not interested, they can go straight to the alternative play activities of their choice. Healthy eating is also promoted, with a snack at each session and cooking activities. Sessions finish with physical play, singing and dancing. This offers an excellent opportunity to emphasise and model the importance of song, rhythm and rhyme in young children's development. There is a safe baby area with toys and recliners for babies to sit and watch the world around them – a comfortable space for parents just to be with their baby. There is also a book area, where children can choose their favourites to look at. Parents are encouraged to read to children, who often cuddle up for a story or two (or three or four).

Helen believes it is essential to make sure that all parents feel really welcome. When a parent and child come for the first time, Helen spends time with them and introduces them to other parents and children to help them feel at home and begin to forge relationships. There is an attractive booklet for parents, which tells them everything they want to know about the group. Specialists from health and education services are invited to the group so that parents have the opportunity to talk with them about key issues. Parental input into how the group is run is seen as central to the group's success, so there is a monthly 'Parents Have Your Say' meeting.

Groups for parents and their babies and toddlers have a variety of names, such as Stay and Play, Baby/Parent and Toddler. They are all groups for parents who stay with their babies and toddlers during a session. Most groups are self-financing, depend on low fees and are run by volunteers.

The Pre-school Learning Alliance provides guidelines and materials to support and extend good practice in running baby and toddler groups. More information is available at www.pre-school.org.uk.

Getting out and about with parents

Local visits with parents

At Maples Children's Centre, London Borough of Ealing, children are taken out on local visits in very small groups. Parents are invited and encouraged to accompany their children. The visits usually stem from the children's interests and needs. They might, for example, involve a short train or bus ride, a walk to the shops, the café, the park, market or local garage. Others might be organised to spot shapes, numbers or print in the local environment. Parents are encouraged to help their child observe the environment; talk about what the children notice; and give their child time to stop, watch and reflect. Digital photos are taken by teachers, parents and by the children themselves.

Digital photography has an immediate impact. Children can look at the photos in the camera; they can be loaded on to the computer as soon as the

> ❞ *I find that going out and about with parents helps me to understand a little more about their lives too.* ❞

group returns to school and shown as a slide show. Children can watch together, remember, recall and retell while events are still fresh in their minds. Parents can be included in this process and enjoy learning how to use the equipment. At Maples, photos are often displayed in the entrance hall the next day on an interactive whiteboard, so that parents can view and discuss them with their children as they enter the nursery. This encourages more parents to make time to accompany their own child on future visits out. Photos can also be put into documents on the computer, with children and parents writing text to describe their experiences. Children and parents can, in this way, together make simple

displays or books. This type of work can be expanded through the loan of digital cameras to parents so that they can take images of their children at home, and be encouraged to use their own local trips to enhance learning. They can record their outings and share their child's interests and experiences with staff in the nursery.

Visits further afield

At South Acton Children's Centre, Ealing, small groups of parents, children and staff (8–10 families) have a day trip to the Science Museum in London. This requires careful forward planning so that parents can arrange time off work or college and get care organised for younger siblings. Places and dates are booked at the beginning of the year so that a specific time in The Garden and Pattern Pod are reserved. The staff have to work hard to seek out and talk to individual parents, establish the value of the outing, and give several reminders of the date and times.

Before the trip, children look at photographs of previous trips to the Science Museum and talk about what they might see and do. Parents are encouraged to come to a preparation session, which is held early in the morning of the same day. Taking only a small group with two members of staff means that the trip is relaxed, with plenty of time for talk. It is not like a traditional 'school outing' but more like a 'family and friends day out'. These visits have been particularly successful in attracting fathers' participation. One member of staff is 'child-free' on the day so that they can mix with parents and children, model positive talking and observation with children, and generally help the day go smoothly. Digital photographs are taken on the journey and inside the museum. These images are displayed the following morning to generate interest and talk as children and parents arrive.

Interests expressed by the children on the day are followed up – for example by planning to make marble runs or patterns or explore shadows. Parents able to come into the setting can be involved in these follow-up activities. Others can take photographs home and recall the trip with their children. Parents say that the visits give them confidence to take children to places such as museums. Many are surprised to find that young children are welcome and that entry is free. An added benefit is the friendships that sometimes develop between parents, having spent the whole day together. Other outings further afield have included trips to urban farms, Heathrow Airport and the Natural History Museum.

Visits out with parents: Childminders

Childminders from *Avon and Somerset Police Constabulary Childminding Network* use visits to local attractions to promote children's learning and development. Parents are invited to at least one event each year. Parents have the opportunity to join in and share their children's experiences first hand, gaining a greater understanding of the 'whole child' and increasing the bond and trust between themselves and their childminder. A day out together provides the opportunity for parents to closely observe childminders engaging children, extending language and thinking skills, as well as expanding knowledge and understanding of the world.

During a trip to Bristol Zoo, the childminders were very aware of the direction of the children's individual interests. They noticed what fascinated and attracted the children and followed this up, encouraging parents to do likewise. Some childminders take digital photographs and load them on to a computer at home for the children to view on a slide show and print off copies to share with their parents. Some of the photos go in the children's 'daily diaries' to share with parents who could not come along on the day.

Sure Start goes wild

Redcar Coast and Dormanstown Children's Centre work in partnership with Tees Valley Wildlife Trust to support children and families in exploring the natural environment. Families and children join the Goes Wild club and they learn how to observe and value wildlife together. Older siblings and extended family members often get involved too. Each month, families are invited to join in a trip or an activity. This might include pond dipping; bird watching; making nest boxes; collecting up litter; planting trees; or visiting local moors, nature sites, beaches, estuaries and butterfly parks. These outings bring families together in a group, where they benefit from shared experiences and build new friendships and relationships.

The Goes Wild club is an ideal opportunity to demonstrate to families how much young children learn through first-hand experience and that valuable learning takes place through simple activities that children enjoy and engage in enthusiastically. It also shows how important the outdoors is for education, as well as helping to establish a love of being outside and of physical activity. Each family is given a pack of resources, which includes items such as a bug box magnifier; pocket guides to birds, insects and flowers; a viewfinder; bug jars; and wildflower seeds. They also get 12 months free membership of the Wildlife Trust with quarterly magazines for parents and children. This encourages the continuation of learning beyond the organised trips as children can read the magazines and use their equipment at home, in gardens and local parks. Parents are surprised to realise they can do so much locally and inexpensively. Many of the sites, although located nearby, are new to the families. Parents report how much they enjoy learning new things for themselves and how they have become more aware of the importance of spending time with their children.

> ❝ *The children are now forever in the garden, looking for signs of life. I can't believe the difference in them.* ❞

Taking learning into homes

Story home visits

At **Maples Children's Centre, London Borough of Ealing,** home visits are made with a story bag containing a picture book and 3D props. These visits are particularly useful in building relationships

with families who may need a little more support to feel confident in accessing other services in the nursery. A key worker walks with a child to their home, listening to the child talking about what they notice along the route and helping to take digital photos. A child's chosen story is shared in the home with parents and sometimes siblings. This is an opportunity to talk about the type of books to borrow from nursery and the most effective style of book sharing. It is also a chance to hear what parents have to say; to learn what they are already doing at home and what books the child has already. Parents who speak a language other than English at home are supported with dual-language texts and given encouragement to speak and read in a child's first language.

Digital photographs are taken of the journey and the home visit. Parents and children can take their own images. These are used to make a picture storybook of the event with captions which the child illustrates, adds writing to and takes home. The storybook and props are left at home for a week and the family are encouraged to continue borrowing more material from a well-stocked lending library, which is available every day. As well as modelling book sharing and giving the chance to encourage parents to build this into a regular daily activity for children, the visit gives an opportunity to discuss many issues and for families to talk about their own concerns, in a calm and relaxed atmosphere.

Parents often enjoy sharing a little of their family history, home languages, photographs and food. Issues around housing, health and family learning needs also arise, and support can be offered through connections with other services. Parents can be encouraged and feel more confident about joining in other workshops, visits and events running in the nursery.

Play-at-Home: Reaching out to families

Redcar and Cleveland has developed a project called Play-at-Home. It involves a series of home visits to children and families with the aim of increasing parent confidence and involvement in their children's play and learning. The families invited to take part are identified as those who are not engaging in other opportunities offered by centres or other local services. Practitioners receive two half days' training, led by the Parenting Coordinator and the Children's Centre Family Link Worker. The training includes an introduction to the structure and content of the Play-at-Home programme and also examines attitudes to parents, the nature of partnership and the importance of parents as educators of their own children. The workers then take play activities directly into children's homes.

> *You can make it fun and enjoy it – before it used to be stressful but now I feel more relaxed.*

> *It has brought the children on lots, especially in their talking.*

The children visited have ranged from two months to four years of age. They receive weekly visits for anything between six to sixteen weeks. The approach is flexible and adapted to individual needs. Each session lasts for around one hour and usually begins with a rhyme or song, followed with a play activity and then a book or story. During the session the workers talk to parents about what the children are doing, pointing out their interests, learning and progress as it is taking place. Each session concludes with feedback from parents, children and practitioners – what has been enjoyed, what might they do next? This supports parents in recognising how they and their children have made progress over the weeks, what they have learnt, likes and dislikes, and so on. Parents are encouraged to choose what play activities they would like to do at the following session and to talk about what activities they have done with their children during the week. Packs of material are left in the home in between sessions so that play and learning can continue.

Some parents feel more relaxed at home and take part without feeling self-conscious about playing in front of other parents and professionals. The visits help to build confidence by taking an individual approach, looking at parents' strengths – the things they do already – as well as the things they would like to change and learn more about. As the weeks go on, and parents begin to feel confident and empowered, the balance gradually shifts and they begin to take the lead on the sessions with support. Parents are also gradually introduced to and encouraged to attend group based sessions within the children's centres and the local community.

> **❝** *My son is starting to play with me more and he wants me to play with him now. Before he didn't.* **❞**

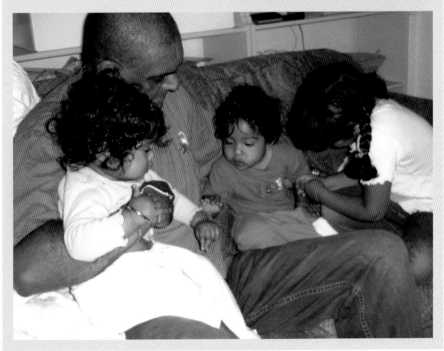

Parents as First Teachers (PAFT)

Parents as First Teachers is an outreach programme offering parent education and family support to families with children aged from pre-natal to five years. The PAFT programme is used by a range of schools and settings to support the work they do with children and families.

The core element of the work is a regular personal visit that lasts for an hour and is usually, but not always, held in the home. On a visit, PAFT-certified project workers share age-appropriate child development information with parents. They help parents to learn to observe their own child's developmental milestones; talk about their parenting concerns; and engage the family in activities that provide meaningful

parent–child interaction, such as making toys and books together. Every visit also involves book sharing. Frequency of visits depends on individual family needs, but is usually monthly.

In addition, parents are invited to group meetings held at the setting and led by project workers or invited speakers. These meetings provide opportunities to share information about parenting issues and child development. The programme is based on a 'strengths model', recognising that one of the parents' strengths is that they are the experts on their child. It hopes to increase parents' feelings of competence and confidence. Project workers also help families to identify and connect with other local services. PAFT trainees have a variety of experience and professional backgrounds. Some parents, who have enjoyed and benefited from the programme themselves, have moved on to train as PAFT project workers.

> ❞ *The visits are excellent as it is a chance to talk to someone about how you feel and how you are doing as a parent.* ❞

More information on PAFT and PAFT training can be found at www.parentsasfirstteachers.org.uk and in the 'Resources' section, page 118.

Involving fathers

Getting fathers involved

When parents first contact **Peter Pan Nursery**, a preschool in Surrey, information and invitations are sent out naming both parents individually. Fathers, and not just mothers, are expected to attend open days; it is considered unusual if they do not. So, right from the start, fathers are actively made to feel included and welcome.

The preschool also holds specific events for fathers. A 'Dads' week' is held during which all fathers are invited into a preschool session of their choosing. Giving this choice of time means that more working fathers are able to negotiate some time away. Attendance is good and the evaluation positive. Many fathers comment that they value the fact they are able to come into a 'female space' together, rather than being the sole man.

> ❝ It was not that easy to get time off work, but absolutely worth it. ❞

Croydon Pre-school Learning Alliance, working with other local early years services, runs a Saturday morning group in a Sure Start centre. The group attracts an average of 15 fathers each week from a range of different ethnic groups and social classes. Most live with their children, although two or three who live apart also attend. Play activities on offer are similar to those that the children would experience during the week in preschool, and practitioners have noted that fathers spend a majority of their time actively engaged and playing with their children. A summer Fathers' Funday event was also held to promote the importance of a father's role in the lives of their children and the following week four new fathers joined the regular Saturday morning group.

> ❝ My little lad is delighted when I say we are going to play school on Saturday and I'm going to stay all morning. ❞

"More fathers now attend Sure Start groups during the week. The word seems to be getting out that we really are a father-friendly place. People may think that a separate group for fathers is exclusive, but we believe it is an important step in helping fathers know that family services exist to serve the whole family and not just mothers with their children."

Dads' Club – sensory garden

Kingsway Children's Centre in Goole set up a Dads' Club so that fathers can give each other support, and feel more confident and comfortable getting involved in caring for their children and helping them learn. It meets weekly, usually during the early evening, so that members can socialise with other male carers and their children. The children's centre Dads' worker attends to support the group and has helped them agree their rules and write a constitution.

The club and staff have planned and planted a sensory garden together, which contains plants that stimulate the senses and are safe for children, including herbs and flowers such as lavender, chives, narcissus and musk mallow. It was researched and planned by Dads' Club members, who like to set up practical projects. They feel this tempts more people to get actively involved, and helps attract new members. Dads' Club members gathered information about plants and began to plan the garden, with one club member taking the lead. An Open Day and barbeque was organised, so that everyone could plant the garden together. They invited their own families, other local families who use the centre, and staff members. This was a great success, and everyone had a wonderful day. Several new members joined the Dads' Club as a result.

Now that the sensory garden is planted, fathers and children are maintaining it together, and beginning to grow vegetables in tubs as well. The skills, knowledge and experience that parents and children have gained are being used at home – for example, some families have taken spare seeds to start growing vegetables. The Dads' Club is planning new projects that include renting a nearby allotment and keeping chickens.

Transition to primary school

Transferring from nursery to primary school

All About Me!

Attach photo or drawing

Name

Date of birth

My Nursery is called

Planning well for transition in partnership with parents can ease a child's entry into Reception class. Activities can be planned over a period of time that will help to reduce stress for a child, enabling them to settle more quickly and to progress in their learning. Support can also be given to parents so that they feel more confident, know what to expect from school and stay engaged in their child's learning. Transition may be particularly difficult for some children, especially those who are just four, are learning English as an additional language or have special educational needs. Settings in the **London Borough of Camden** have found that clear transition support plans for some of these children (combined with Individual Education Plans for special educational needs) are particularly useful. Meetings with parents, staff from existing and receiving settings, and other relevant professionals, can be invaluable in the formation and execution of the plan. To help parents and children prepare they also:

- Share and lend home picture storybooks about starting school to encourage discussion of issues such as playtime, older children, lunch times and separate boys' and girls' toilets.

- Make videos of Reception classes to show children and parents.

- Visit new schools with families, taking photos together of new staff, entrances, toilets, the playground, and children working and playing (these can then be made into displays or books to borrow for home).

- Encourage discussion, using puppets, about going to a new school.

- Visit the new classroom 'in action' together with families or invite Reception teachers back to the nursery; arrange for nursery children to visit a few times for short sessions – perhaps joining in at lunch or storytime.

The **Camden Early Years Intervention Team** has developed a book – *All About Me*.* for key persons, parents and children to discuss and complete. Children are helped to reflect and record their feelings, memories, likes and dislikes. The book is then ready to go to their new school.

All About Me is available for download on the PEAL website and on the CD-ROM included in PEAL training packs. Note: See also 'Little learners at home – transition to nursery' on page 101.

8 Learning from PEAL

PEAL was researched, designed and piloted by a small project team and delivered at large regional training events by the team and a pool of PEAL trainers. The associate trainers have become an integral part of PEAL in many ways, and they have contributed reflections on their experience. This section outlines some of the learning from the design and delivery of PEAL, and considers its impact, using trainers' words to illustrate the key points.

The content of any training is clearly critical, but PEAL has demonstrated to all those involved the vital importance of the way that content is communicated. The nature of the training itself and the way in which it was delivered has had a positive effect on the experience of both participants and trainers. As one trainer reflected:

> "The interesting thing about PEAL is not just the direct work but also the processes and the way you have developed a team (in the broadest terms) and shared a journey that is open, reflective, creative, energetic and fun. These organisational lessons are very interesting and valuable. I am also sure that this learning will be of value to wider NCB and other PEAL partners, perhaps not least the DCSF too. The challenge is to institutionalise strong values in the way we work and I think the PEAL story has something good to contribute. Often the gap in our work is not to 'know what' to do, but to 'know how' to make something real and of value to people in the real world."

The PEAL journey

Early planning

The original task of producing materials and training for early years practitioners raised a number of challenges. The team was asked to reach practitioners in 700 children's centres in its first year. It was decided that between two to four practitioners from each setting would be invited to spend up to a day in preparation, attend a facilitated training day, and then take ideas from the training back to their settings. This form of 'cascade' training in itself has not always proved to be a successful strategy for ensuring the consistent delivery of a programme of learning, or the embedding of that learning into future day-to-day practice. What became clear in early discussions was that successful delivery would depend on several essential components: the provision of high quality materials to underpin cascaded sessions; the involvement of managers and leaders; clarity in both the objectives and outcomes and the route to delivering these; and well prepared, skilled and supported trainers who would feel inspired by PEAL's messages and, in turn, inspire practitioners.

The design

The challenge was then to produce materials that could offer a diverse group of trainers enough consistency and guidance on delivery, with clear learning outcomes, and provide participants with high quality, accessible material that included examples of effective practice and training sessions that could be adapted for local delivery. The content of the training was firmly grounded on both research and practice evidence about what works best in involving parents in their children's early learning. The team were guided in this by suggestions from a highly experienced Advisory Group.

The design of PEAL was informed by sound training and learning theory. This included Kolb's (1984) cycle of experiential learning and learning styles, Honey and Mumford's (1982) work on preferred learning styles, and the work of those writing about organisational learning and learning organisations, such as Burgoyne and Senge (Pedler and others 1991; Senge 1990).

"I learned so much from PEAL about course design, the thought process, the flow and last but not least the importance of well presented training materials."

"Because of the prior work and research that had gone into the programme it felt supporting and real."

"The matching of training skills with the PEAL materials offered participants the best of both worlds – emphasising that the process of learning and the experience of sharing ideas is an essential part of good training."

The delivery

The intention was to build a 'learning community', to learn continuously from all those involved as developers, deliverers and participants in the training, and to make use of that learning in further resources and developments.

Feedback from participants and trainers, from both pilots and roll-out sessions was considered and acted upon to keep the training materials relevant and up to date:

"It has not stayed still – it has enhanced and to some extent reinvented itself."

"What I love about PEAL is it's a two-way, organic process. The group is supported by the trainer to learn and reflect, and at the same time the trainer gets to hear about some excellent practice as well as consider the value of the exercises and learning outcomes."

"New trainers have been recruited to widen and diversify the team. New types of work have been added to offer workshops to childminders, the private and voluntary sector and local authorities. Materials have been extended and rewritten for new audiences. Case studies and practice examples have been added to, addressing new scenarios and situations."

The training process modelled the approach and values advocated in the training itself – not telling people 'how to do things' but working in partnership with participants, exploring the materials and messages together, and modelling a welcoming, facilitative approach. There was a consistency between the way participants were treated on a training day and how parents should be treated in settings.

"This was at the core of PEAL, from the good communications to the welcome of participants at workshops to the respect and value shown to people in the choice of venues and the support offered."

"I have learned that successful projects must focus on both the process and the outcomes equally and do this in partnership with everyone."

At larger events a 'lead trainer' was often on hand, free from the responsibility of leading a training group, but available to meet and greet latecomers and offer the training in a small group until it was possible to join a specified group at a break.

"Sometimes we deliver a catch up session for people who arrive late. This enables them to rejoin a group by first break without disrupting the flow of an established group. It is another of the ways PEAL shows how it values people. These catch-up sessions can be a slightly unusual experience – sometimes running the first session with only one or two people. They can be intense. But people appreciate the personal touch and it gets them up to speed on the activities and research."

"Latecomers often fed back how bad they felt about arriving late but how quickly this was overcome by the way they were greeted and introduced to their training group."

Finally, the need to include managers in the training was addressed through encouraging managers and heads of centres to attend the training with members of their team, and to sign an agreement that they would release staff for preparation activities. Training was developed in the second year aimed directly at local authorities, so that early years advisors and those in more strategic roles were also included.

Recruiting and supporting trainers

Trainers were recruited through national advertising, according to essential criteria that included considerable experience in delivering participative training. This brought in trainers with a rich range of experience including those who had been involved with early years through working in local authorities or through related services where work with families had been the focus, such as mediation, health and mental health services, disability equalities work, domestic violence and work with young parents. The depth and variety of experience brought strengths to the team and trainers learned from each other.

"The trainers are a diverse bunch with many different experiences. PEAL made a decision to go with effective trainers and facilitators in the first instance."

"There are many experienced people in the PEAL team and I have learned much from them. I think we have all borrowed approaches and ideas from each other. Seeing the way different trainers run an exercise, or the way they introduce a particular topic has been very beneficial. Everyone has a personal style and approach. As a member of the PEAL team I never felt isolated or on my own. I always felt I could gain ideas, advice and energy from other members of the team. I also got a lot from each trainer as they linked the PEAL ideas to their own experiences and work – showing how working with parents adapts to a variety of settings across the UK."

"Meeting other trainers was another highlight – such a varied group of people! I found the sheer variety of their work and life experiences fascinating and inspiring."

"As for my colleague trainers, I was staggered by the breadth of people, their skills and talents … Being with the PEAL team and trainers was a treasure box of learning. From reading Jackee's book 'Soul Purpose' to chatting to Paul about being a Non-Executive Director to hearing Helen speak with passion about the PEAL research, all these had untold impact on my personal development."

PEAL 'Training the Trainers' days were held where appointed PEAL associates worked to understand the training materials, and practice delivery. The trainers were provided with 'trainers' packs' which included the resources, handouts and practical items for delivery. The initial training was followed by an opportunity to shadow a more experienced trainer. This shadowing proved to be one of the most appreciated and successful strategies for preparing trainers to deliver their own sessions. The trainers welcomed this level of investment in their development – and it helped establish real commitment to PEAL. (Shadowing was not available to the very first trainers in the early sessions – who acted as very successful 'trailblazers'!)

"The training for trainers ... dispelled all my fears about delivering someone else's material and in fact got me to the point where I truly believed that what we were about to do was worth doing and would make a difference to the lives of children."

"Train the trainers was a good starting point where a lot of things were explained. With shadowing and reading they became clearer and clearer and when the first training event took place it was not so stressful and I felt comfortable doing it."

"Joining other trainers for induction felt safe and comfortable, particularly with a couple of experienced trainers ... sharing their personalised approaches and practice. The combination of a 'running commentary' on the materials and activities, whilst also having the opportunity of working through the PEAL training programme, provided a comprehensive package and contrasts extremely favourably with other experiences of induction for delivering training."

"It was very clear they wanted PEAL to be successful and they wanted it to change people's lives. I wanted to be a part of it."

"With the rosy glow of hindsight I began to appreciate the need for consistency of message and emphasis on evidence-based practice when I subsequently realised just how many PEAL trainers there were and how important it was for all participants to have a high quality experience and receive a 'uniform' programme."

"Watching someone else deliver the day is just amazing. Not only do I get to see how the whole thing knits together (especially the research), but also watch someone else's training style: how they manage the group; deal with situations; respond to the needs of participants; etc. No matter how many times I've trained, I always learn something from watching someone else."

Throughout the training roll-out, trainers were kept in touch by regular e-mail contact, telephone discussions, briefing papers, website entries and the provision of updated materials. Issues arising from the training delivery were fed back to the core PEAL team through trainer evaluation forms. These were picked up at development days where trainers met, received updated information, and debated and discussed key issues.

"It has been good to keep in touch with the team by e-mail. There has been a good exchange of ideas and discussions. This virtual networking has enabled a group of people who live and work across the breadth of England to keep in touch and maintain a sense of team."

> *"It was good to build relationships with the other trainers. And I feel lucky that PEAL was willing to invest in us as a group through training, networking and several CPD days … PEAL is different because it values the team ethic and the importance of trainers working together."*

> *"The development days were also useful as it gave us an opportunity to reflect on our experiences, to share with other trainers and PEAL team and to learn something new."*

> *"I felt that the PEAL team cared about us as trainers and never did this become a doubt."*

> *"From the outset … you felt that there really was no such thing as a silly question and that your own personal skills, knowledge and experience were valued."*

> *"Early in my PEAL experience it became clear that the project was designed to get the most out of the team."*

> *"I never felt like a commodity to PEAL – I feel like a person who is valued and who is known."*

This sense of building a valued team, a 'learning community', was extended beyond the trainers to all new partners and to those joining to help at events, develop the website, work on the evaluation or help run the office. All were included and involved in experiencing the training at first hand as part of their induction so that they developed some understanding of its aims and approach.

Impact

The trainers have also commented on the impact of PEAL on their own development, and they have some interesting observations on how participants responded on training days.

Trainers' journeys

> *"Another interesting aspect is that this training enabled me to move away from my usual field (refugees and migration) and opened some new possibilities for me."*

> *"What have I learned from PEAL? The power of the research messages about informal learning and how to get these across in direct, clear ways that empower parents. The importance of teamwork. That role-play can be totally redefined as a positive experience for everyone (participant, facilitator and observer)."*

"I have recently agreed to become an assessor for those attending the training wishing to pursue accreditation, so I am pleased that my journey will continue for a while longer. It's been a fantastic year: I've learnt, I've shared, I've guided, I've been guided. I've developed my own confidence and hopefully those of my trainees. I can't wait to see those accreditation portfolios."

Participants' journeys

"I will never forget one participant from that workshop. She was an 18 year old who was just starting out … and this was the first workshop she had ever been to … She was nervous and unsure of herself – even though she had some colleagues with her. She found it difficult to talk in the group at first. During the discussions of parents and home learning she started to share her thoughts. From then on she was contributing more than anyone – and offering some real insights into the experience of being a young practitioner and looking for ways to build confidence and skills with parents. You could also see other participants start to acknowledge and value her. PEAL had unlocked something for this young woman – it was wonderful to watch."

"Over the last year and a half there have been many people who have stuck in my mind. The experienced practitioner … who had the courage to stand up in front of the group and admit she always doubted her ability to engage with parents. The man in London who described how he engages dads from the moment they come in to the centre. The group of four practitioners who told me they 'knew it all' about engaging parents and then were challenged by others in the group when they demonstrated by their contributions they did not. The workers … who described the way they worked on the streets of their local community to meet and talk to local parents. The woman … who came to me during first break to ask how to work with 'bad parents'. She then came back to me in the afternoon to say that she had thought hard about her views and had decided that labelling parents as 'bad' was not very helpful and she needed to rethink some of her core beliefs. The group … who were so passionate about the PEAL research they were going to work with parents to produce a leaflet on it. The staff member in a setting who used to be a parent there. She was able to talk about the gap that sometimes occurs between what staff believe is in place in terms of parental involvement and how it actually feels to the parents."

Learning into action

This section concludes with some thoughts on evaluation. An evaluation of the second roll-out of PEAL training is being conducted by the NCB Research and Evaluation department. This will be available on the PEAL website when published.

PEAL feedback forms from participants confirmed that the vast majority of participants (95 per cent) had found PEAL training useful and that it had met, and frequently exceeded their expectations. However, all those involved in the delivery of the events were keen to find out if anything would really change as a result of the training. All too often, when practitioners return to the day-to-day realities in settings, it proves impossible to put into practice what has been learned. As one trainer noted:

"As a facilitator, delivering PEAL always left me with a rosy glow. However, at the end of every day there was a sense of disappointment that I wouldn't see whether it really made a difference. I was therefore delighted when two things happened. First of all participants had the opportunity to achieve accreditation and secondly I was able to work with practitioners to develop practice examples."

Practitioners who had previously attended PEAL training were offered workshops to support them in preparing learning portfolios for accreditation. Trainers attending the workshops in the role of mentors and assessors were delighted to learn of the way real changes had been inspired by the training and to hear some of the ideas that had taken shape. One extract from an accreditation portfolio is included here to illustrate this:

"One reason I talked to Hannah's Nana is because I just felt more comfortable with her. But I realise that even if children have 'prickly' parents, the children still have the same needs, and it's just as important – maybe even more so – to build up relationships with their families. The PEAL training day did help me realise this. I did those practice conversations on the day, and I think I need more practice, so I am going to ask my manager if we can do that activity ourselves sometime. Meantime, I am going to pay more attention to the parents I find most 'difficult' and make sure this doesn't stop me from trying to get them involved."

A number of trainers have also worked alongside settings as they developed new parent-partnership projects after attending PEAL training. Most of these will be summarised and published on the website as new examples of practice. Some have already been included in Section 7 of this book, and four additional extracts are highlighted below, which demonstrate how PEAL has had a direct influence on practitioner thinking and action. The full texts, and other examples, can be viewed on the website (www.peal.org.uk).

Little Learners at home – transition to nursery

Sherwood Children's Centre, Newark and Sherwood, Nottinghamshire, run 'Little Learners' transition groups for two to three-year-old children and their parents. They attend a two-hour session once a week for a term, before entry to nursery. Observations on development and learning are regularly shared at these sessions with parents, and are then used to inform future planning of the

sessions and next steps for individual children. Digital photos are also taken by the children and adults during a session and these are either displayed on a 'Little Learners' display board or in the child's portfolio. The portfolios also contain drawings, paintings, examples of early writing and so on. Working in this way has already enabled practitioners to build confidence in listening and talking with parents and the resulting positive relationships mean that parents often make the first move and discuss their child's development and any concerns.

Following PEAL and Listening to Young Children training* the centre identified the need to give parents more support for learning at home with their child and to develop ways of capturing parents' own observations of what their child was saying and doing. Activity packs for parents and children to use between sessions were developed. The importance of listening to children as they play is emphasised and a home portfolio provided for parents and children to compile together. In this way, parents have become more deeply involved in observing their child's interests and play over the week, and now share this knowledge with practitioners at the next group session. The packs include items such as storybooks with a game and ideas for imaginative play; construction activities; collage and cutting sets; dough recipes; and modelling materials. A laminated card is included in each pack, giving information on ideas for play and explaining what a child will be practising and learning.

*Lancaster and Broadbent (2003).

All Wrapped Up – reaching out to families

Armley Moor Children's Centre in Leeds set up a small, targeted project to reach out to children and families. The key aims were to encourage certain families – particularly fathers – who were not already involved in their child's learning at the setting to develop confidence, share observations and make more use of free local resources.

Some of the children involved were included because they showed relatively low levels of well-being and involvement. The name of the project – All Wrapped Up – is intended to signify the emotional security and relationships everyone hoped to foster and develop between families and the centre and between children and families. The centre worked with just six families at first; in each family a father or another significant male agreed to take part. The families and two practitioners visited The Royal Armouries, a museum in Leeds, every week for a period of six weeks – to explore materials and resources. Each visit had a theme such as 'Fur and Feathers' or 'Metal'.

Initial discussions took place with families, explaining the project, encouraging them to take part, and ensuring individual needs and circumstances were taken into account to maximise participation. Most parents were very pleased to be asked to be part of something special. The initial preparatory discussions were essential as they established real commitment and interest in the project and helped relationships develop; practitioners also got to know more about the challenges some parents face and more about individual children's learning and behaviour at home. After the outings, parents and children were supported to do follow-up activities. These included printing out digital photographs and compiling 'a memory box' and book of the visits (including collected items, photos, children's drawings and so on). Creative activities related to each trip also took place, and these sessions were open to all families.

Sharing observations with parents – digital cameras

At **Stanlaw Abbey Community Nursery, Cheshire**, practitioners wanted to make more use of digital cameras to increase and enliven the two-way sharing of observations with parents. A computer was placed near the entrance with photos on a slide show, showing children at play in the nursery – so that parents can see and talk about what their children have been doing. Children and parents stop to look at the computer as they arrive and talk about the photos. The process has generated lots of discussion about learning.

The nursery staff then decided to lend cameras to parents and children so that they could take their own photographs, bring them back to the nursery and talk with their key carer about what they had been doing at home. It was decided to launch this idea with a special project based around a nursery bear. The bear, who is called Stan, was designed and chosen by the children at a visit to a bear factory. Stan now visits a child's home for the weekend or a few days to play and join in everyday activities with the family. Parents know that Stan likes having stories read to him and he wants to be included in everything. Parents and children make notes for Stan about his stay and take digital photos. The photos are shown and discussed with other children and key carers at group time when the bear returns. Practitioners now know a lot more about families and about children's individual interests and activities at home. This information is used in planning at the setting. Both parents and practitioners feel more confident in initiating conversations about individual children's learning.

Home visits with story sacks

Camrose Children's Centre in Northampton set up a story sack corner for children, parents and staff. A party was held in the centre to celebrate World Book Day at which Bookstart treasure chests were distributed and the story sacks were introduced. Home visits were then arranged at a convenient time for families. Children chose a sack when they arrived at the centre for the session and then, when parents returned to collect their children, the child's key worker accompanied them home with the sack where the story and contents were shared together. The sacks contain picture books, rhymes, props, puppets, games, factual books, CDs and jigsaws – all related to the theme of the main storybook. The story sacks were left at home so that the story and activities could be repeated.

Families across the children's centre – from the nursery, baby and toddler room, and drop-in and play centres – have been visited. A series of six workshops for parents are now being planned around play activities in the home and nursery. They will build on the relationships started by the home visiting project, and it is hoped that more parents will feel confident to attend, having already been visited at home.

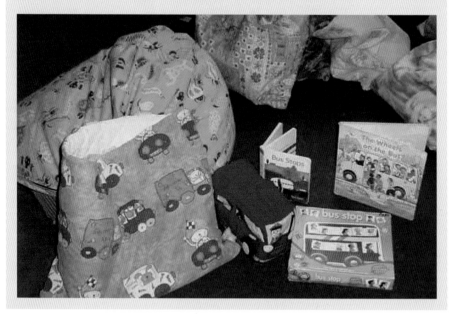

9 Next steps

This final section provides a few ideas that might act as useful starting points for further learning, reflection on practice and action.

1. Think about what your setting already does with parents

Use the self-evaluation questions in Appendix 2 ('What does your setting do with parents already?'). This form has been taken from the PEAL *Activities* booklet that participants are asked to read and complete before attending a PEAL training day. It provides a useful way to examine and evaluate current practice. It could be used by a practitioner working alone, or discussed with a colleague – or, perhaps most effectively, with a whole staff team.

After recording what you already do, and thinking about your evidence, you could consider how your colleagues' reactions compare with yours, what areas you feel are strengths for your setting and for your own practice, and what needs development.

2. Talk to parents in your setting

Finding out what parents feel and think is helpful. How do parents actually perceive and make use of the provision for involvement in learning? Asking parents how they are made to feel and what they think can produce some surprises. Participants on PEAL training have found that some parents are actually unaware of what practitioners thought were well known and easily accessible opportunities to engage in learning in their settings. Suggested starting points for parent questions and interviews can be found in the PEAL *Activities* booklet – 'Activity 6: What's it like being a parent here?' This booklet can be downloaded from the PEAL website (www.peal.org.uk).

3. Start a project, no matter how small

Read through the PEAL practice examples. Extracts are included in this book and they are available in full in the PEAL pack (and many are also on the website). Find an idea that particularly interests and inspires you, investigate it further, and develop it in a way you feel is appropriate for your parents, children and community. If you do this, please write to the PEAL team via the website and tell us about your work.

4. Use PEAL training exercises in your setting

The PEAL *Training Guide* contains several exercises that can be repeated in settings. For instance, 'Session 7: Communication and confidence', in which participants practise everyday conversations with parents, taking the role of either parent or practitioner, in a revolving carousel.

This exercise helps a team practise communication skills, articulate practice and policies, and provides the opportunity to learn how others manage conversations with parents. It gives a chance to reflect on how it feels to be a parent in the setting. It also leads, through discussion, to certain important learning points – in particular, the need to listen actively to parents and other colleagues.

Practitioners remark, after taking part in the carousel, on how they often feel they must keep talking, explaining and finding solutions for parents, when in fact, listening actively, reflecting back to parents what they are saying, asking them for ideas, and negotiating is often more effective.

Typical feedback comments include:

> *"I probably talk more than I listen, even though I thought I was a good listener!"*

> *"I've learned it is OK not to know all the answers. It is OK to question practice and say you'll ask others or find out more."*

> *"I really noticed people's 'body language' – how you stand and if you look like you're really interested – this all matters doesn't it?"*

Links are readily made from this exercise to the Parent Adviser partnership model described in Section 5 – Equal partnership.

5. Go on further training

Take up opportunities for further training and reflection. PEAL training is now available from the Early Childhood Unit of the National Children's Bureau. Local authorities can arrange PEAL training for practitioners, advisors and trainers. A list of other training providers can be found in the 'Resources' section on page 118.

Appendix 1:
PEAL practice example: Home visits

Home visits

It is established practice in many centres to visit families at home before children start at a setting. It helps to begin forming the relationship between parents, practitioners and children; and starts the process of sharing information.

> *Mandy came to visit Hannah at home. It really helped. She knew her when she started nursery and I felt more certain that she would be well cared for.*

There are real benefits to visiting children in their homes more often. It can be particularly useful in reaching families who, for a variety of reasons, find it hard to take up opportunities offered within the setting.

Why do more home visits?

Parents and children often feel more relaxed in their own home, and parents appreciate having time to talk on a one-to-one basis. It helps to develop a relationship and build trust in a more relaxed environment. After a home visit, parents often feel more confident in approaching a practitioner with comments and questions. The closer relationship may also mean families are more inclined to take part in the workshop sessions, events and trips offered by the setting.

Children always remember and talk about a home visit long after the event; it is a special occasion in their lives and enhances the practitioner–child relationship. Digital photographs can be taken of the visit (with permission) and used, with the child, to recall the event.

Seeing a child in their home environment can also help to explain certain behaviour patterns and interests.

At school, Yasir seeks out adult company actively and prefers this to playing with other children. He loves to help with cleaning and sorting tasks. Visiting him at home helped his key worker to understand that his role as a much younger sibling in a large family means that he spends most of his time with older children and adults, joining in with what they do.

Home visits help to break down stereotypes as practitioners gain knowledge about varied family practices, cultures and histories; they learn that all families are very different. Having greater knowledge about a child's home and family also enables a practitioner to 'tune in' to the child and have more meaningful conversations. This is particularly useful for children who have speech and language needs or who are in the very early stages of learning English as an additional language.

During a visit, practitioners can discover what learning activities are already taking place in the home – whether the child has favourite books, likes particular videos, goes out on visits, cooks regularly. And information may be gathered on who else might be able to support home learning – fathers, grandparents, older siblings, other relatives.

At nursery Pali, who is acquiring English as a second language, often speaks about members of his family, but staff find it hard to understand what he is saying. He also talks a lot about the number 8 and clearly recognises the numeral. By walking with him to his house, taking photographs and talking to his mother, his key worker was able to find out the names of the people who live in his flat and understand their relationship to him. She also discovered that he lives on the 8th floor and likes to press the button himself for the lift. 'This my house (8), this my car (G – ground floor).'

Home visits can be used to model positive interaction, working together with parents and children to re-tell stories, play games, sing rhymes or listen to stories on tape in the home language.

A game, activity or tape can be used; or started and left with the family to repeat or complete. Videos of children playing in the nursery can be watched together and discussed; then left with the family to share.

Parents can also be supported to think through how to manage certain aspects of behaviour at home, and strategies can be planned between home and the setting.

> Amina's mummy was very reluctant to borrow books from the library. She said she cannot look after them, all books get destroyed by her younger children. She has three children under four and is on her own with them most of the time. Amina's key worker visited her at home. They talked through ways to help, finding a special place for the book bag to be kept and deciding on one special time when mummy would read the book with Amina and her younger brother after their meal. Practitioners also talked to Amina at nursery, with her mummy, about books and how to care for them; they made a point of asking Amina each morning if she had her book bag and would she like a new book.

Things you may need to consider!

There will be some families who will not want a home visit and this should be respected. You may repeat the offer at a later date, once you have built a trusting relationship. Also consider offering a one-to-one meeting in the setting instead.

It's important to plan home visits well. Plan the route and how you will travel. Allow enough time for each visit so that you don't feel rushed. Take telephone numbers with you. Tell the family who to expect in advance of the visit and the time you will arrive. Plan and gather equipment to take with you, for example something for the child to

play with; a story bag or maths game to share; and a digital camera.

It's important to be friendly and relaxed, making the experience enjoyable – be prepared to adapt and be flexible. Parents must feel confident that you are not there to judge them. You may benefit from training before visiting or from accompanying more experienced colleagues at first.

Rather than asking lots of prepared questions, share some information about yourself, news about the centre, listen to parents and children carefully, and follow up on what they say and ask.

Try to be sensitive to cultural differences – for example, some families will appreciate it if you offer to take your shoes off before walking into their house. Always ask permission before you take photographs.

It is likely that you will be offered drinks and even food. People feel good about being able to offer you something. Think about what your approach to this will be. Televisions are often left on during the day at home, even when visitors arrive. Think about how to approach this. It can be best to settle in a little first, and then ask for it to be switched off before you start any activity with a child. Think in advance how you will phrase this request.

You will need to adhere to your setting's health and safety procedures for home visits. For example, you may not wish to visit homes alone. If possible, ask for support staff or even volunteers to assist you.
Before they can assist, however, their CRB checks must be completed and they must have been informed about issues of confidentiality and child protection. There should be a record kept at your setting of where practitioners go and what time they are expected back and you may be encouraged to carry a mobile phone.

See practice examples: Story home visits, Settling in and Time to talk.

We find some parents are much more relaxed and open when discussing their child at home.

peal

Ideas combined from the experience of parents and practitioners in early years settings.

Appendix 2:
What does your setting do with parents already?

Resource sheet 1.1 from Parents, Early Years and Learning Activities booklet

What does your setting do with parents already?

The terms *mothers and fathers* and *parents* are used here to mean all male and female parents and carers of children who are in a primary carer role in a child's life.

We know the make-up of our local community and families well *(e.g. ethnicity, languages spoken, religion practised).*
We are approachable and welcoming to mothers, fathers and families.
We have a clear 'settling in' strategy – when both children and parents are actively helped to settle into the setting.
Our physical space is designed to encourage parents to spend time in the centre.
A member of staff leads on parental involvement in learning and actively works to promote it.
All children have a key worker or person who gets to know families.
Key workers know and use parents' first names *(with permission).*
Mornings and/or going-home times are structured to give extra time for parents to discuss their children when they arrive/leave.
Key workers have the opportunity to visit children at home before entry.
Key workers have the opportunity to visit children at home on other occasions throughout the year.
Parents have open access to records of children's learning. They are parent-friendly and easy to understand.
All parents sometimes share their own observations of what children say and do at home.
All parents **regularly** share their own observations of what children say and do at home.
Parents' observations of children are used to plan future learning in the setting and at home.
We discuss with parents the best ways of including and involving disabled children.
Parents are given informal support for their children's learning at home *(e.g. occasional book borrowing).*
Parents are given more regular support for learning at home *(e.g. activities/equipment regularly shared between home and setting).*
Resources are attractive and accessible to all parents and children, and reflect a wide range of families and experience.
Parents are offered workshops/courses to help them support children's learning.
We monitor who borrows material, attends workshops, shares observations *(e.g. we would know if a particular ethnic group is not participating).*
We have strategies in place to try reaching parents who are not taking part in what is offered.
We have good knowledge of where to find support for our parents locally *(e.g. English as additional language classes, housing advice).*
Parents are involved in offering training and information to other parents about children's learning.
We have a clear 'transition' strategy – to support children and parents moving on to Reception.

We do this already	This is developing	We need to do more	How do I know/demonstrate this?

Source: Wheeler, H, Connor, J (2006)

Appendix 3: The PEAL team

Working group

Sue Owen, Director of the Early Childhood Unit, National Children's Bureau
Bernadette Duffy, Head of Centre, Thomas Coram Children's Centre
Lucy Draper, Head of Coram Parents' Centre, Coram Family
Barbara Sampson, Head of Early Years and Sure Start, London Borough of Camden

and from 2007–08:
Julie Hathaway, National Childminding Association
Tim Kahn, Pre-school Learning Alliance
Angela Gibbons, National Day Nurseries Association

Project team

Joyce Connor, Project Manager, Principal Officer, Early Childhood Unit
Helen Wheeler, Senior Development Officer, Early Childhood Unit
Heather Goodwin, Administration and Training Coordinator, Early Childhood Unit
Keith Phillips, Associate Lead Trainer
Sindi Hearn, Events and Technical Assistant

and from 2007–08:
Liz McIntyre, Development Officer
Ashley Duke, Administrator
Faye Hounsome, Administrator
Beki Hawes, E-Publishing Assistant
Paulina Filippou, Communications Officer

PEAL trainers

Rose Bailey
Jeanne Barcsewska
Regina Bash-Taqi
Kim Bevan
Eileen Blezard
Carol Bushell
Kay Crosse
Paul Cutler
Mary Devlin
Audrey Dorival
Philip Douch
Pam Gallagher
Judith Gibson

Rachel Gillett
Liz Greer
Cathy Hamer
Jacqui Heap
Jude Holby
Jackee Holder
Alison John
Joanna Marshall
Y. Penny Lancaster
Andrea Layzell
Suzanne Leckie
Barbara Lisicki
Beba Parker

Hilary Penny
Melissa Pereira
Claudine Rane
Jane Reynolds
Maxine Roake
Jasbinder Rooprah
Carleen Schofield
Jeanne Soddy
Shirley Stansfield
Fiona Weir
Delroi Williams

Advisory group 2005–07

Dame Gillian Pugh, Chair, formerly Chief Executive, Coram Family

Professor Lesley Abbott, Manchester Metropolitan University

Janet Ackers, Foundation Stage of the Primary National Strategy

Cath Arnold, The Pen Green Centre for Under Fives and Families

Mary Crowley MBE, Parenting UK

Jenny Deeks, ContinYou

Jean Jackson, Parenting UK

Y. Penny Lancaster, Coram Family

Anne Longfield, 4Children

Stephanie Mathivet, Pre-school Learning Alliance

Sally Mehta, Parentline Plus

Joan Norris, High/Scope

Maggie Reid, Parent at Thomas Coram Children's Centre

Usha Sahni, Ofsted

Peter Silva, Peers Early Education Partnership (PEEP)

Purnima Tanuku, National Day Nurseries Association

Lynne Taylor, National Childminding Association

Phillippa Thompson, 4Children

Bev Grant, DfES (until September 2005)

Michael Collins, DfES (until December 2005)

Kathryn Dowling, DfES (until June 2006)

Jennifer Robson, DfES

Our thanks also go to the late Professor Sheila Wolfendale for her contribution to the Advisory Group and support of the project.

Other contributors

Thank you to those who read draft copies of the original training materials and made suggestions for additions and changes:

Mary Dickins, All Together Consultancy

Jane Lane, Advocate worker for racial equality in the early years

Patrice Lawrence, Lead on Race Equality for NCB

Barbara Lisicki, Barbara Lisicki Trainers Ltd, Creative disability and diversity consultancy and training

Iram Siraj-Blatchford, Professor of Early Childhood Education, Institute of Education

Thank you also to those who read drafts or draft extracts of this book:

Cathy Hamer

Patrice Lawrence

Sue Owen

Keith Phillips

Dame Gillian Pugh

Barbara Sampson

Iram Siraj-Blatchford

We are also very grateful to the following who shared their experience and provided examples of practice and photographs.

The Camden Early Years Foundation Stage Advisory Team:
Susan Kalirai
Carol Archer
Neena Chilton
Danielle Smith

The Camden Early Years Intervention Team:
Shelagh Alletson and Beth Harding, project workers on the Early Years and Parents Project

Laura Gould, Senior Child Care Worker, Coram Parents' Centre, Coram Family

Armley Moor Children's Centre, Leeds
Beeches Pre-school, Peterborough
Camrose Children's Centre, Northampton
Collingham Gardens Nursery, Camden
Coram Fields Nursery, Camden
Dove Children's Centre, Wolverhampton
Gamesley Early Excellence Centre, Derbyshire
Holly Lodge Playgroup, Camden
Kingsway Children's Centre, Goole
Konstam Children's Centre, London Borough of Camden
Maples Children's Centre, London Borough of Ealing
Norfolk Children's Services
PAFT, Parents as First Teachers
PEEP, Peers Early Education Partnership
Pen Green Centre for Under Fives and Families, Northamptonshire
Ready, Steady, Go Nursery, Camden
Redcar and Cleveland Adult and Children's Services
Seacroft Children's Centre, Leeds
Selby Children's Centre, North Yorkshire
Sherwood Children's Centre, Newark and Sherwood, Nottinghamshire
South Acton Children's Centre, Ealing
Stanlaw Abbey Community Nursery, Cheshire
Sure Start, Battersea
Sure Start, Redcar Coast and Dormanstown Children's Centre
Thomas Coram Children's Centre, London Borough of Camden
York Rise Nursery, Camden

References

Athey, C (1990) *Extending Thought in Young Children: A Parent–Teacher Partnership*. London: Paul Chapman.

Blanden, J (2006) *'Bucking the Trend': What Enables Those Who are Disadvantaged in Childhood to Succeed Later in Life?* Working Paper No. 31. London: Department for Work and Pensions.

Brooker, L (2002) *Starting School: Young Children's Learning Cultures*. Buckingham: Open University Press.

Carr, M (2001) 'Assessment in early childhood settings: Learning stories', in *Assessing Children's Learning*. New Zealand Council for Education Research (NZER) (training pack).

Davis, H, Day, C and Bidmead, C (2002) *Working in Partnership with Parents: The Parent Adviser Model*. London: The Psychological Corporation.

Department for Children, Schools and Families (2007) *The Children's Plan: Building Brighter Futures*. London: DCSF.

Department for Education and Skills (2002) *Birth to Three Matters: A Framework to Support Children in Their Earliest Years*, Literature Review. London: DfES.

Department for Education and Skills (2003a) *Every Child Matters*, Green Paper. London: DfES.

Department for Education and Skills (2003b) *The Skills for Life Survey: A National Needs and Impact Survey of Literacy, Numeracy and ICT Skills*. Research Brief 490. London: DfES.

Department for Education and Skills (2007) *The Early Years Foundation Stage: Setting the Standards for Learning, Development and Care for Children from Birth to Five*. London: DfES. (revised 2008)

Desforges, C with Abouchaar, A (2003) *The Impact of Parental Involvement, Parental Support and Family Education on Pupil Achievements and Adjustment: A Literature Review*. Research Report 433. London: DfES.

Draper, L and Duffy, B (2006) 'Working with parents', in Pugh, G (ed) (2006) *Contemporary Issues in the Early Years*, fourth edition. London: Sage Publications pp.151–162.

Early Childhood Forum (2005) *Participation and Belonging in Early Years Settings. Inclusion: Working Towards Equality*. London: National Children's Bureau.

Easen, P, Kendall, P and Shaw, J (1992) 'Parents and educators: Dialogue and development through partnership. *Children and Society*, 6, 4, pp.282-296.

Equalities Review (2007) *The Final Report of the Equalities Review*. London: The Cabinet Office.

Feinstein, L (1999) *Pre-School Inequality? British Children in the 1970 Cohort*. London: Centre for Economic Performance, University College.

Goldman, R (2005) *Fathers' Involvement in Their Children's Education*. London: NFPI.

Hannon, P (1995) *Literacy, Home and School: Research and Practice in Teaching Literacy with Parents*. London: Falmer Press.

Harris, D and Spencer, J (2000) 'Barriers to parental involvement in nursery, playgroup and school' in Early Years Trainers Anti-Racist Network (2000) *Partnership with Parents: An Anti-discriminatory Approach*. Wallesey, Cheshire: EYTARN.

Honey, P and Mumford, A (1982) *The Manual of Learning Styles*. Maidenhead: Peter Honey.

Hughes, AM (2006) *Developing Play for the Under Threes: The Treasure Basket and Heuristic Play.* Milton Park: David Fulton Publishers Ltd.

Kolb, DA (1984) *Experiential Learning: Experience as the Source of Learning and Development.* New Jersey: Prentice-Hall.

Laevers, F (1997) *A Process-oriented Child Monitoring System for Young Children. Leuven,* Belgium: Leuven University.

Lancaster, YP and Broadbent, V (2003) *Listening to Young Children.* Buckingham: Open University Press.

Leitch Review of Skills (2006) *Prosperity For All in the Global Economy: World Class Skills.* Final report. London: The Stationery Office.

Moran, P, Ghate, D and van der Merwe, A (2004) *What Works in Parenting Support? A Review of the International Evidence.* Research Report 574. London: DfES.

National Evaluation of Sure Start (2006) *Outreach and Home Visiting Services in Local Sure Start Programmes.* Report 017. London: DfES.

National Literacy Trust (2001) *Parental Involvement and Literacy Achievement: The Research Evidence and the Way Forward. A Review of the Literature Prepared by the National Literacy Trust.* Consultation Paper. London: NLT.

Nutbrown, C (2006) *Threads of Thinking: Young Children Learning and the Role of Early Education.* London: Sage Publications.

Nutbrown, C, Hannon, P and Morgan, A (2005) *Early Literacy Work with Families.* London: Sage Publications.

Page, J and Whiting, G (2007) *Engaging Effectively with Black and Minority Ethnic Parents in Children's and Parental Services.* Research Report 013. London: DCSF.

Pedler, M, Burgoyne, J and Boydell, T (1991) *The Learning Company.* London: McGraw-Hill.

Pen Green Centre for Under Fives and Families (2004) 'All about ... working with parents', *Nursery World,* 3 June, Supplement, pp.15–22.

Peters, M, Seeds, K, Goldstein, A and Coleman, N (2007) *Parental Involvement in Children's Education Survey.* Research Report 034. London: DCSF.

Pre-school Learning Alliance (2005) *Fathers Matter.* Leaflet. London: PSLA.

Pugh, G and De'Ath, E (1989) *Working Towards Partnership in the Early Years.* London: National Children's Bureau.

Quinton, D (2004) *Supporting Parents: Messages from Research.* London: Jessica Kingsley Publishers.

Roberts, A and Featherstone, S (2002) *The Little Book of Treasure Baskets.* London: Featherstone Education Ltd.

Sammons, P, Sylva, K, Melhuish, E, Siraj-Blatchford, I, Taggart, B, Grabbe,Y and Barreau, S (2007a) *Influences on Children's Attainment and Progress in Key Stage 2: Cognitive Outcomes in Year 5.* Effective Pre-school and Primary Education 3–11 (EPPE 3–11). London: University of London, Institute of Education, DfES.

Sammons, P, Sylva, K, Melhuish, E, Siraj-Blatchford, I, Taggart, B, Barreau, S and Grabbe, Y (2007b) *Influences on Children's Attainment and Progress in Key Stage 2: Social/Behavioural Outcomes in*

Year 5. Effective Pre-school and Primary Education 3–11 (EPPE 3–11). London: University of London, Institute of Education, DfES.

Sammons, P, Sylva, K, Melhuish, E, Siraj-Blatchford, I, Taggart, B, Barreau, S and Grabbe, Y (2008) *The Influence of School and Teaching Quality in Children's Progress in Primary School*. Effective Pre-School and Primary Education 3–11 (EPPE 3–11). London: University of London, Institute of Education, DCSF.

Seaman, P, Turner, K, Hill, M, Stafford, A and Walker, M (2006) *Parenting and Children's Resilience in Disadvantaged Communities*. London: National Children's Bureau for the Joseph Rowntree Foundation.

Senge, P (1990) *The Fifth Discipline: The Art and Practice of the Learning Organisation*. New York: Doubleday.

Siraj-Blatchford, I (2004) 'Educational disadvantage in the early years: How do we overcome it? Some lessons from research. *European Early Childhood Education Research Journal,* 12, 2, pp.5-20.

Siraj-Blatchford, I and Manni, L (2007) *Effective Leadership in the Early Years Sector: The ELEYS Study*. London: University of London, Institute of Education.

Siraj-Blatchford, I and McCallum, B (2005) *An Evaluation of Share at the Foundation Stage, Final Evaluation Report*. London: Institute of Education.

Siraj-Blatchford, I, Sylva, K, Muttock, S, Gilden, R and Bell, D (2002) *Researching Effective Pedagogy in the Early Years*. London: DfES.

Siraj-Blatchford, I., Sylva, K., Taggart, B, Sammons, P, Melhuish, E and Elliot, K (2003) *Intensive Case Studies of Practice Across the Foundation Stage*. Technical Paper 10. London: University of London, Institute of Education, DfES.

Sylva, K, Melhuish, E, Sammons, P, Siraj-Blatchford, I and Taggart, B (2004) *The Effective Provision of Pre-School Education (EPPE) Project: Final Report*. London: DfES and Institute of Education, University of London.

Sylva, K, Melhuish, E, Sammons, P, Siraj-Blatchford, I and Taggart, B (2007) *Promoting Equality in the Early Years: Report to The Equalities Review*. London: University of London, Institute of Education.

Tunstill, J, Meadows, P, Akhurst, S, Allnock, D, Chrysanthou, J, Garbers, C and Morley, A (2005) *Implementing Sure Start Local Programmes: An Integrated Overview of the First Four Years*. NESS Summary SF010. London: DfES.

Whalley, M and Arnold, C (1997) *Parental Involvement in Education: Summary of Research Findings*. London: Teacher Training Agency.

Whalley, M and the Pen Green Team (2001) *Involving Parents in their Children's Learning*. London: Paul Chapman Publishing.

Wheeler, H and Connor, J (2006) *Parents, Early Years and Learning: Reader*. London: National Children's Bureau.

Whitehead, MR (2004) *Language and Literacy in the Early Years*. London: Sage Publications.

Williams, B, Williams, J and Ullman, A (2002) *Parental Involvement in Education*. Research Brief 332. London: DfES.

Further training

Parents, Early Years and Learning (PEAL)

PEAL is available to local authorities and other organisations through the Early Childhood Unit of the National Children's Bureau and is accredited through City and Guilds. More information is available at www.peal.org.uk

There is a range of providers of training for practitioners to support and enhance parental involvement in early learning. Those listed below all contributed material to PEAL or were referenced in the PEAL *Reader*.

Pen Green Centre for Under Fives and Families

The centre provides training and accreditation with Leicester University and the University of Northampton, and a quality assurance scheme on their approach to involving parents in their young children's learning – Parents Involved in their Children's Learning (PICL). The programme consists of an initial two days training, project work in settings, followed by a further day's training. All participants receive comprehensive training materials and a video.

More information is available at www.pengreen.org or by phoning 0153 644 3435.

Peers Early Education Partnership (PEEP)

PEEP provides a two-day training course and packs of materials for practitioners who wish to develop their work with parents around children's learning (0–5 years) and become more familiar with the PEEP approach and material. PEEP focuses on working in partnership with parents to enhance children's learning, building self-esteem and positive attitudes to learning, all through effective communication and warm relationships. Material is provided for five age levels: babies, ones, twos, threes, and fours. Each level has a Learning Together folder of activities, a video, a songbook and CD for parents to use at home.

More information is available at www.peep.org.uk or by phoning 0186 539 7974.

Parents as First Teachers (PAFT)

PAFT offers a five-day training course, with a follow-up day six months later, for practitioners on implementing and using the PAFT family support programme and material with parents and children (0–5). The training focuses on personal visits, group meetings, developmental milestones, and community resources, as well as child development and parenting information.

More information is available at www.parentsasfirstteachers.org.uk or by phoning 0184 434 5847.

Share at the Foundation Stage

Share is a family learning programme led by ContinYou. It offers facilitator training for practitioners in working with parents and resource packs with suggestions for workshops and activities that parents can use at home to support their child's learning through active experience and play.

More information is available at www.shareuk.org.uk or by phoning the Family Learning Team on 0247 658 8440.

Working in Partnership through Early Support

The Early Support programme and material supports families and practitioners in the effective coordination of information and services for young children with disabilities or special educational needs. An accredited training course is also available to enhance partnership working. The course has three units, each of which is supported by a day of training, distance learning, assessment activities and a tutorial. The content looks in depth at the Early Support approach to partnership, including key working. For managers who do not need accreditation, there is also a two-day course on Working in Partnership.

More information is available at www.earlysupport.org.uk

The Pre-school Learning Alliance

The Working with Fathers – Including the F-word...(That is, Fathers) workshop aims to explore some of the reasons why few fathers and other male carers appear to get involved in early years settings. It invites participants to reflect on the barriers to father involvement and suggests strategies for developing effective ways to involve fathers. The workshop ideally takes four hours but can be tailored to suit the needs of participants. More information is available by phoning 0207 697 2500.

The *Learning Together Facilitator Programme* is a two-day training for those who want to deliver family learning programmes through workshops. There is an opportunity to become familiar with activities from the Looking at Learning Together family learning course. More information is available by phoning 0207 697 2505.

Fatherhood Institute

The Fatherhood Institute offers a range of courses to help agencies support fathers' relationships with their children. These are delivered over one, two or three days in central locations or can be delivered in-house. They include Working with Fathers in Early Years; Working with Difference: Engaging Fathers in Multi-cultural Communities; Women Working with Fathers; and Working with Young Fathers. Some courses are accredited. More information is available at www.fatherhoodinstitute.org

Other providers

Information on providers of training to support work with parents in their wider parenting role can be found at the National Academy for Parenting Practitioners (NAPP) (www.parentingacademy.org).

A full list of other training providers and approaches that were demonstrated as part of the Early Learning Partnerships Project (ELPP) can be accessed at www.familyandparenting.org/ELPP

Additional support for parents

A

Adoption UK
http://www.adoptionuk.org
Helpline 0844 848 7900

Al-Anon Family Groups
http://www.al-anonuk.org.uk
Helpline 0207 403 0888
Helpline and support groups for families affected by alcohol misuse.

Alcohol Concern
http://www.alcoholconcern.org.uk/servlets/home
A website with a wide range of information about alcohol.

Alcoholics Anonymous
http://www.alcoholics-anonymous.org.uk
Helpline 0845 769 7555

B

BBC website
http://www.bbc.co.uk/skillswise
The Skillswise website has been developed to help adults improve their reading, writing and maths skills. Interactive activities are aimed at Level 1 of the Basic Skills Literacy and Numeracy Curriculum.

C

Children's Disability Information
http://www.childrensdisabilities.info
An information website providing articles and resources for parents of children with disabilities, with particular focus on special needs.

Citizens Advice Bureau
http://www.citizensadvice.org.uk
This service helps people resolve their legal, money and other problems by providing free information and advice from local centres.

Contact-a-Family
http://www.cafamily.org.uk
Helpline 0808 808 3555
Contact a Family provides advice, information and support to the parents of all children with disabilities.

D

Disabled Parents Network

http://www.disabledparentsnetwork.org.uk

Helpline 0870 241 0450

Information and support for people with disabilities who are parents or who hope to become parents and their families, friends and supporters.

Drinkline

Freephone 0800 917 8282

Alcohol misuse advice line.

E

Equality and Human Rights Commission

http://www.equalityhumanrights.com

Main telephone line 0845 604 6610

Textphone 0845 604 6620

Information and guidance on discrimination issues.

G

Gingerbread

http://www.gingerbread.org.uk

Freephone 0800 018 5026

Support and information for single parents.

H

Homestart

http://www.home-start.org.uk

Freephone 0800 068 6368

Offers a local service – home visits, support, friendship and practical assistance to families.

L

Learndirect

http://www.learndirect.co.uk

Helpline on 0800 101 901

Advice and information on learning and careers. The service is aimed at those with few or no skills and qualifications who are unlikely to participate in traditional forms of learning. Advice is available in a range of languages.

N

Narcotics Anonymous
http://www.ukna.org
Helpline 0845 373 3366
Support and advice on drug addiction.

National Family and Parenting Institute
http://www.e-parents.org
The parents' website offers information and guidance on behaviour, food, family law and health services.

National Society for the Prevention of Cruelty to Children (NSPCC)
http://www.nspcc.org.uk
Helpline 0808 800 5000

NSPCC Asian Helpline
Bengali 0800 096 7714
Gujurati 0800 096 7715
Hindi 0800 096 7716
Punjabi 0800 096 7717
Urdu 0800 096 7718

P

Parenting UK
http://www.parentinguk.org
Telephone 0207 284 8370
Information on local parenting classes.

Parentline Plus
http://www.parentlineplus.org.uk
Freephone 0808 800 2222
Information and support on all parenting issues. Local parent groups are also organised for mutual support.

R

Refuge
http://www.refuge.org.uk
Freephone 0808 200 0247
Help in dealing with domestic violence.

Refugee Action

http://www.refugee-action.org.uk

Telephone 0207 654 7700

Information and advice for asylum-seekers and refugees.

Refugee Council

http://www.refugeecouncil.org.uk

London Advice Line 0207 346 6777

Yorkshire and Humberside Advice Line 0113 386 2210

East of England Advice Line 0147 329 7900

West Midlands Advice Line 0121 620 1515

The Refugee Council gives help and support to asylum seekers and refugees. The
network of regional offices offer one-stop services.

S

Shelter

http://england.shelter.org.uk

Freephone 0808 800 4444

Information and advice on housing problems.

Index

self-confidence, parents 40, 87, 88, 103
self-evaluation 105, 110–11
SEN 10, 14, 47
sensory garden 90
settings 4, 43–4
    barriers to 19–20, 53–4
    evaluation of 105, 110–11
Settling-in – Getting to know children and families (PEAL practice example) 36
Share at the Foundation Stage 119
'Sharing our stories' 37
Sherwood Children's Centre 101
singing/songs 9, 66, 74, 79
Siraj-Blatchford, I 30, 43, 44, 49
Siraj-Blatchford, I and McCallum, B 12, 49
Siraj-Blatchford, I and Manni, L 43
Skills of Life Survey (DfES) 19
social class 9, 10, 19
social development 9, 11, 14, 51
social support 85
socio-economic issues 10, 11, 17–18, 19, 52–3
songs/singing 9, 66, 74, 79
South Acton Children's Centre 69, 81
special educational needs 10, 14, 47
Stanlaw Abbey Community Nursery 103
Statutory Framework 6–7
'stay and play' groups 79
stereotypes 30
Stop! Look! Listen! 60–1
story-telling 50–1, 66, 70
    story home visits 85, 104
study sessions, for parents 63, 74
support
    for learning 6, 44–7, 101
    social 85, 121–4
Sure Start Church Street, Westminster 78
Sure Start Battersea 74
Sure Start programmes 55
Sylva, and others 9, 10, 14, 43

T
take-home packs 47, 65, 66, 68, 69, 70, 72, 74, 101, 103
Tees Valley Wildlife Trust 83
Thomas Coram Children's Centre 18, 35, 46, 47, 64, 73
Time to talk (PEAL practice example) 36, 45
toy libraries 71, 76
training
    of practitioners 86, 99–100
    of trainers 48, 96–9
    see also academic achievement; PAFT; PEAL

transition
    to nursery 101
    to primary school 91
treasure baskets 76
Treasureboxes 65
Tunstill, J and others 27, 28
two-way observations 44–7

U
under threes 76–9

V
video 68
visits (outings) 9, 47, 80–3, 102, 103
    see also events; home visits

W
websites 118–24
welcomes 52–6, 74, 79, 89
Wellholme Park Children's Centre 76–7
Whalley, M and Arnold C 63
Whalley, M and Pen Green Team 13, 17, 20, 21, 30, 53
'What activities create a strong home learning environment' 49
'What stops involvement?' (Research sheet 2) 21
Whitehead, MR 52
wildlife 83
Williams, B and others 17, 21
working hours 18, 19
Working in Partnership Through Early Support 119

Y
York Rise Nursery 65